PSHE and Citizenship

Key Stage 1

Judy Hunter and Sheila Phillips

Published in 2002 by:
Nelson Thornes Ltd
Delta Place
27 Bath Road
CHELTENHAM
GL53 7TH
United Kingdom

02 03 04 05 06 / 10 9 8 7 6 5 4 3 2 1

A catalogue record for this book is available from the British Library

ISBN 0-7487-6396-1

Illustrations by Alex Machin, Sally Michel and Sue Swales
Page make-up by GreenGate Publishing Services

The authors and publishers wish to thank the following for permission to use copyright material:
Material from the *English Non-Statutory Guidelines for PSHE and Citizenship Key Stages 1 and 2* is Crown copyright reproduced with the permission of the Controller of Her Majesty's Stationery Office.
Material from the *Scottish Health Education 5–14 Guidelines* is copyright of the Queen's Printer and Controller of HMSO and is reproduced with the permission of the Queen's Printer for Scotland.
Material from *Personal and Social Education Framework: Key Stages 1 to 4 in Wales* © Qualifications, Curriculum and Assessment Authority for Wales (ACCAC) 2000.
Material from the *Northern Ireland Guidelines on RSE for Key Stages 1 and 2.* Copyright © The Northern Ireland Council for the Curriculum, Examinations and Assessments (CCEA).
Learning outcomes reproduced from *Passport: A framework for personal and social development* by Jane Lees and Sue Plant by courtesy of the Calouste Gulbenkian Foundation (tel. 020 7636 5313)

Every effort has been made to trace the copyright holders but if any have been inadvertently overlooked the publishers will be pleased to make the necessary arrangement at the first opportunity.

Printed and bound in Great Britain by Ashford Colour Press

Contents

Everything I needed to know I learned in Kindergarten

'Most of what I needed to know about how to live and what to do and how to be, I learned in Kindergarten. Wisdom was not at the top of the Graduate School mountain, but there in the sandbox at Nursery School. These are the things I learned.

Share everything. Play fair. Don't hit people. Put things back where you found them. Clean up your own mess. Don't take things that aren't yours. Say sorry when you hurt somebody. Wash your hands before you eat. Flush. Learn some and think some and play and work some, every day. When you go out into the world, watch for traffic, hold hands and stick together. Be aware of wonder. Remember the little seed in the plastic cup. The roots go down and the plant goes up and no-one really knows how or why, but we are all like that. Goldfish and hamsters and white mice and even the little seed in the plastic cup – they all die.

Everything you need to know is in there somewhere. Ecology and politics and sane living. Think what a better world it would be if we all – the whole world – had a basic policy to always put things back where we found them and clean up our own messes. And it's still true, no matter how old you are, when you go out into the world, it is best to hold hands and stick together.'

(Robert Fulghum, Grafton Books, 1989)

Introduction

This resource

This resource is designed to cover the requirements of the curricula and guidelines for England, Wales, Scotland and Northern Ireland. Charts matching the content of this resource to the relevant documents can be found on pages ix–xvii.

Activities within this book are based on the belief that to make healthier choices, to develop respect, to play an active role as citizens, to act responsibly, children need more than information alone. They need the skills to use the information they learn and the self-esteem/sense of self-worth to put what they might know into practice. We have included some material for skill development and raising self-esteem within this resource and, in addition, schools can use further material to enhance this aspect of their programme and ensure a balanced approach.

An emphasis on skill development and raising self-esteem at Key Stages 1 and 2 lays the foundation for the more detailed information which follows at Key Stages 3 and 4 – it puts the building blocks in place:

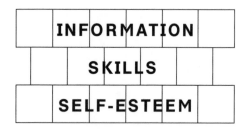

The cement which holds the blocks together is the opportunity for children to see a model for PSHE and citizenship within their lives – to live it, to reflect upon it and to learn from it. School councils and forums are one example. Topics/aspects of PSHE and citizenship need to be revisited through a *spiral curriculum* approach, that is a planned curriculum which reviews, consolidates and extends children's understanding and skills and allows them to assimilate knowledge when it is appropriate to their age, their maturity and their ability.

The notion of a spiral curriculum demands that we also take the time to review what children know and understand and what their perceptions

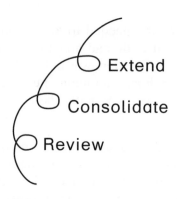

are, otherwise many of the messages we are trying to impart, many of the skills we are trying to develop, are lost. Children see the world very differently from adults. The Draw and Write technique developed by the Health Education Unit at Southampton University is an excellent technique for establishing children's perceptions and we recommend it to you.

This model of delivery fits comfortably with the overall goal for citizenship as documented in Education for Citizenship in Scotland:

'Education for citizenship should aim to develop capacity for thoughtful and responsible participation in political, economic, social and cultural life. This capacity is rooted in knowledge and understanding, in a range of generic skills and competencies, including 'core skills', and in a variety of personal qualities and dispositions. It finds expression through creative and enterprising approaches to issues and problems.

Being a capable citizen is not just about possessing knowledge and skills. It is about being able and willing to use knowledge and skills to take decisions and act. Nor is effective citizenship just about having the capacity and disposition to be active. It is about being able to take action and make things happen for ends – and by means – that are infused with respect and care for people and a sense of social and environmental responsibility.

Finally, capability for citizenship, as envisaged here, includes ideas about 'political literacy'. It also encompasses social, economic and cultural 'literacies' coupled with the capacity for participation in all aspects of society – political, economic, social and cultural.'

The Framework for PSHE and citizenship at Key Stages 1 and 2 as published in *The National*

Curriculum Handbook for primary teachers in England (1999), states that children should gain the knowledge, skills and understanding to:

1   develop confidence and responsibility and make the most of their abilities.
2   prepare to play an active role as citizens.
3   develop a healthy, safer lifestyle.
4   develop good relationships and respect the differences between people.

A whole school approach

Whilst this book focuses on topics/aspects which are specific to PSHE and citizenship, it is not intended to be seen or used in isolation from other opportunities that form a whole school approach. PSHE and citizenship is a way of 'being' with children, it is a modelling of the relationships and behaviours we are seeking to develop in them, it is a way of bringing the learning to life, it is about respecting children and involving them in their learning. The activities chosen as a focus for specific work are important, as are the processes happening within the classroom and within the whole school environment. PSHE and citizenship is about maximising planned learning opportunities through the curriculum as a whole.

The need to 'model' and 'bring alive' citizenship is summed up by the following:

'Education for citizenship is more than a simple expectation of political literacy. Civics lessons are not enough. The ethos of the school must be conducive to good citizenship.'

(Douglas, Osler, *Education for Citizenship in the New Scotland*, Gordon Cook Foundation, 1999)

Similarly, the Welsh Personal and Social Education Framework states:

'A whole school approach to PSE will incorporate a range of experiences to promote the personal and social well-being of children and young people and enable them to develop a sense of self-worth and relate effectively to others. PSE will equip them to be more informed, confident and skilled in order to take an active and responsible part in society and it will enhance learning, motivation, performance and achievement.'

The National Healthy School Standard (NHSS) was launched in October 1999 and is jointly supported by the Department for Education and Skills (DfES) and the Department of Health (DH). It advocates a whole school approach,

focuses on school improvement issues and supports schools in the development of PSHE and citizenship.

Teaching and learning styles

A range of teaching strategies needs to be used to provide all children with learning opportunities and we have endeavoured to offer a range within this resource. PSHE and citizenship does, however, lend itself particularly to active learning, discussion work, enquiry and participation in 'real life' projects, and teachers will be able to extend material to take this into account. Many messages can be reinforced through assembly work.

Circle work is an excellent methodology for building a classroom environment where children can develop skills and self-esteem, and many teachers will be familiar with its processes and structure. In facilitating the process of children developing their own ground rules, understanding the importance of equality in the circle, learning to listen and take turns, negotiate issues and reach consensus on decision making, teachers are providing a model of PSHE and citizenship 'in action'.

Outside agencies and visitors can enhance programmes and complement the work of teachers. However, attention needs to be given to how a school ensures that visitors' values and philosophies are compatible with those of the school. Time needs to be spent planning together and reviewing together.

Involving parents/carers

Effectively involving parents/carers in the education of their children can be a difficult task and yet they are often the greatest influence in a child's life. A school's task is to educate the citizens, the workforce, the parents of tomorrow and to do that they may well also need to educate the parents of today. Involving parents/carers in PSHE and citizenship education can have two functions: it can enhance children's educational experiences and it can also be a means of educating their parents/carers. Where appropriate we have suggested ways of involving parents/carers through some of the pupil activities.

Assessment, recording and reporting

Children (and their parents/carers) have the same right to know how they are progressing in PSHE and citizenship as they do in any other aspect of the curriculum. Self-reflection/assessment and the ability to begin to set targets for him or herself is an important part of a child's development and should be seen as an integral part of the PSHE and citizenship programme. In the *PSHE and citizenship Framework* we are given two broad areas for assessment:

- Children's knowledge and understanding, for example information on health, understanding of rules, understanding of health and safety procedures, and the meaning of ideas, including democracy.
- How well children can use their knowledge and understanding in developing skills and attitudes, for example through participating in discussions, group tasks and activities, managing conflict, making decisions and promoting positive relationships.

Within the framework we are also told:

'Assessment in PSHE and citizenship should not imply that children are failing as people or citizens. It should not be a judgement on the worth, personality or value of an individual child or their family. This can be particularly important to working with children from diverse backgrounds or children who have emotional and behavioural difficulties. A record of children's progress and portfolios of work will provide evidence for reports to parents that might include their child's awareness of topical events, exercise of responsibility and contribution to the life of the school.

Schools may wish to recognise children's achievements in PSHE and citizenship by awarding their own certificates. These could be linked with a school's system of commendations.'

In looking at your PSHE and citizenship curriculum, in conjunction with other curriculum areas, the learning outcomes for Key Stage 1, as detailed in *Passport: A framework for personal and social development*, commissioned by Calouste Gulbenkian Foundation, can prove a useful tool. These learning outcomes are on pages xviii–xxi.

Themes/Aspects

We have incorporated the *aspects* or *themes* of the Frameworks/Guidelines for England, Wales, Scotland and Northern Ireland and divided this resource into activities which cover the following:

- Looking good and feeling well
- Growing and changing
- Medicines and drugs
- Keeping safer
- Eating and exercise
- Feelings and feeling good
- Friendships, families and me
- The environment
- Citizenship
- Reviewing progress

How to use this book

Both the teacher's notes and the activity sheets are intended to be used with the minimum of preparation and additional resources. The activity sheets are photocopiable. The length of lessons/activities may vary as schools will have differing amounts of time to devote to PSHE and citizenship and will choose to deliver their programmes in different ways. There is a helpful checklist at the back which will help in developing and reviewing your programmes of study.

Where you see we have suggested some children's books which you may find useful to enhance your work and which can be incorporated into your literacy teaching. Literature can provide an excellent means of exploring some of the issues that children often find difficult to talk about and of developing a language which enables children to express their emotions. Children can be encouraged to discuss issues through the characters and this is often more comfortable for them than talking about themselves directly.

England Curriculum Guidelines

Knowledge, skills and understanding	Key Blueprints Units
Developing confidence and responsibility and making the most of their abilities	
1 Pupils should be taught:	
a to recognise what they like and dislike, what is fair and unfair, and what is right and wrong	24, 35, 37
b to share their opinions on things that matter to them and explain their views	24, 35, 42
c to recognise, name and deal with their feelings in a positive way	23–26
d to think about themselves, learn from their experiences and recognise what they are good at	27, 28, 36, 45
e how to set simple goals.	32
Preparing to play an active role as citizens	
2 Pupils should be taught:	
a to take part in discussions with one other person and the whole class	Throughout
b to take part in a simple debate about topical issues	24, 41, 42
c to recognise choices they can make, and recognise the difference between right and wrong	24, 35–37, 42
d to agree and follow rules for their group and classroom, and understand how rules help them	11, 35, 36
e to realise that people and other living things have needs, and that they have responsibilities to meet them	26–28, 36, 39, 46
f that they belong to various groups and communities, such as family and school	28, 31–33, 38–40, 42, 46

Preparing to play an active role as citizens (continued)

g	what improves and harms their local, natural and built environments and about some of the ways people look after them	31–34, 38
h	to contribute to the life of the class and school	11, 31, 33, 42
i	to realise that money comes from different sources and can be used for different purposes.	31, 33, 38, 39, 41

Developing a healthy, safer lifestyle

3	Pupils should be taught:	
a	how to make simple choices that improve their health and well-being	1, 7, 10, 14, 16–19, 43, 45
b	to maintain personal hygiene	21–22
c	how some diseases spread and can be controlled	10, 22
d	about the process of growing from young to old and how people's needs change	2–6
e	the names of the main parts of the body	
f	that all household products, including medicines, can be harmful if not used properly	7–9, 15
g	Rules for, and ways of, keeping safe, including basic road safety, and about people who can help them to stay safe.	9, 11–14, 15, 45

Developing good relationships and respecting the differences between people

4	Pupils should be taught:	
a	to recognise how their behaviour affects other people	22, 24, 26, 27, 35, 36, 38
b	to listen to other people, and play and work co-operatively	19, 24, 26–28, 35, 36, 39, 42, 46

x

c	to identify and respect the differences and similarities between people	2, 26, 40, 44
d	that family and friends should care for each other	27, 28, 30, 39, 40
e	that there are different types of teasing and bullying, that bullying is wrong, and how to get help to deal with bullying.	24, 36

Breadth of opportunities

5	During the key stage, pupils should be taught the knowledge, skills and understanding through opportunities to:	
a	take and share responsibility (for example, for their own behaviour; by helping to make classroom rules and following them; by looking after pets well)	1, 9, 11, 13, 14, 17, 24, 26, 28, 32, 34–40, 42
b	feel positive about themselves (for example, by having their achievements recognised and by being given positive feedback about themselves)	23, 25, 27–30, 32, 40
c	take part in discussions (for example, talking about topics of school, local, national, European, Commonwealth and global concern, such as 'where our food and raw materials for industry come from')	3, 7, 9, 11, 12, 14, 30, 31–34, 38, 39, 41, 42
d	make real choices (for example, between healthy options in school meals, what to watch on television, what games to play, how to spend and save money sensibly)	17, 20, 24, 31, 32, 35, 40, 42
e	meet and talk with people (for example, with outside visitors such as religious leaders, police officers, the school nurse)	4, 5, 11, 15, 18, 20, 35, 39
f	develop relationships through work and play (for example, by sharing equipment with other pupils or their friends in a group task)	Throughout
g	consider social and moral dilemmas that they come across in everyday life (for example, aggressive behaviour, questions of fairness, right and wrong, simple political issues, use of money, simple environmental issues)	12, 23, 24, 26, 30–37, 39, 42
h	ask for help (for example, from family and friends, midday supervisors, older pupils, the police).	8, 12, 14, 18, 27, 28, 30, 36, 37, 40

Scotland – Health Education 5–14 National Guidelines

Key Stage 1 match to *Blueprints PSHE and Citizenship*

Strand	Level A	Level B	Level C
Physical health This strand explores physical factors in relation to our health and looking after ourselves	• Show an awareness of ways of keeping healthy through, e.g. eating and drinking, exercise, sleep, keeping clean and brushing teeth **1, 16, 20, 21**	• Show their knowledge and understanding of what individuals need to do to be healthy, e.g. varied diet, regular exercise **5, 10, 17–19, 21**	
	• Show an awareness of simple ways of keeping safe, e.g. safe use of medicine **7, 8**	• Identify a range of ways of keeping safe, e.g. avoiding substances, and practising safe food preparation and safe road use **9, 11, 12, 13, 14**	
	• Show an awareness of the way their bodies grow and change **2, 3, 4, 6**	• Recognise ways in which individuals are unique, e.g. height, eyesight **29**	
Emotional health This strand explores emotions, feelings and relationships and how they affect our mental well-being	• Recognise their own feelings about themselves and towards others, e.g. know when they feel sad or happy **23**	• Recognise a range of feelings they, and other people, experience at different times, e.g. feelings of fear, excitement **26**	• Use personal and interpersonal skills to relate to other people **40**
	• Recognise that their families and other special people in their lives care	• Communicate with others through a developing vocabulary	• Identify strategies to help deal with loss and grief **25**

Social health This strand explores the interaction of the individual, the community and the environment in relation to health and safety		
• relating to emotions and feelings, e.g. being able to talk in simple terms about how they feel **25, 30** for them and help them **28**	• Recognise the value of family and friendships **28** • Show an awareness of caring and sharing, e.g. taking turns **24, 27**	• Identify the ways in which people care for them **28** • Show how they respect and care for themselves and others **27, 29**
• Show safe ways of dealing with a range of situations, particularly those that may present risk, e.g. bullying **36**	• Identify ways in which the local environment can affect their health, e.g. traffic, smoke **33** • Show simple ways of keeping the environment clean, safe and healthy **31, 32**	• Show an understanding of how they can contribute responsibly to their community, e.g. avoiding creating litter **35, 39, 41, 42**
	• Identify ways in which they can contribute to keeping their environment clean, safe and healthy **34, 38** • Show simple ways of getting help, e.g. telling, dialling 999 **12**	• Show ways of getting help, e.g. in the event of an accident or a bullying incident **36, 37** • Show simple ways of avoiding incidents, e.g. approaches by people they do not know, crossing the road safely **15**

Wales Curriculum Guidelines

Personal and Social Education Framework	
Knowledge and understanding	**Key Blueprints Units**
Social aspect	
Know how to be a good friend	27–30
Understand the variety of roles in families and the contributions made by each member	27–30
Community aspect	
Know about the variety of groups to which they belong and understand the diversity of roles that people play in those groups	28, 32, 35, 38
Understand that they can take on some responsibility in their friendship groups	27, 28, 32, 36
Physical aspect	
Understand that medicines are taken to make them better, but that some drugs are dangerous	7–9
Know that exercise and hygiene and the right types and amount of food are important to keep their bodies healthy	1, 5, 10, 14, 16–22
Know about the dangers from the road, being near water and other threats in the home and the environment	9, 13, 15
Know what to do or to whom to go when feeling unsafe	11, 13, 15
Sexual aspect	
Know the names of the parts of the body in order to distinguish between male and female	
Distinguish between appropriate and inappropriate touching	12
Emotional aspect	
Begin to understand the range of feelings and emotions in different situations	23, 24
Be aware of their own feelings	24, 25
Understand that other people have feelings and know what affects them	23, 24, 26
Spiritual aspect	
Know that each person is different but understand that all are equal in value	29, 40
Understand that people have different preferences, views and beliefs	40

Moral aspect	
Understand that rules are essential in an ordered community	35, 38, 39
Know what is fair and unfair and what they believe to be right and wrong	24, 37
Vocational aspect	
Know about the different jobs and workplaces in the community	39
Understand that money can buy goods and services and is earned through work	39, 42
Learning aspect	
Know what they are good at	29
Understand how they can improve their learning	
Environmental aspect	
Know about the features in their local environment	31–34, 38, 39
Understand how their environment could be made better or worse to live in and how they can make a difference	31–34, 38, 39

Northern Ireland Curriculum Guidelines

Guidance for Primary Schools: Relationships and Sexuality Education	Key Blueprints Units
Myself	
• Myself, how I grow, feed, move and use my senses; caring for myself, for example hygiene, sleep, exercise	1–5, 10, 16–22
• Naming parts of the body (basic), developing an agreed language for our bodies	6
• Being myself, I am unique, my self-esteem, self-confidence, independence, respect and caring for myself	5, 11, 14, 22, 29, 30
• Similarities and differences between myself and others, for example uniqueness, fingerprints, gender issues, different rates of growth	2, 3, 5, 6, 23, 29
• An introduction to the stages of human development, changes as we grow, for example baby, child, teenager, adult, mother/father, grandparents	2–6
• Recognising moods, feelings and concerns and developing a language and an appropriate manner of expressing them, for example What do I do if I feel sad or angry?	7, 11, 23–28, 30, 41
• Personal likes and dislikes	
My Relationships	
• My family, special people in my life. What they do for me and what I do for them	27–30, 39, 40
• Friendships, getting on with each other, for example communicating, playing together, listening, co-operating and sharing	24, 26–28, 30, 31, 35–42
• Ageing, how do we know that things are alive, dead, young and old	2

• Loss and mourning, death of a person or a pet. (Note: the situations of the pupils should be taken into account prior to introducing this topic.)	25, 26
• Respect and caring for family members and friends, for example caring for a new baby	2, 4, 27, 28, 30
• Bullies and what to do about them	12, 35–37
• Personal safety, simple skills and practices to maintain personal safety	8, 9, 11, 13, 15, 33
• The difference between good and bad touches	12, 35–37
• Realise that adults and older children are not always friends; the potential danger of relationships with strangers or acquaintances	8, 12, 15, 36, 37
• Strategies which pupils might use to protect themselves from potentially dangerous situations	9, 11, 14, 15, 33

My Community/Environment

• Awareness of different types of families and the roles of individuals within families	30–32
• Keeping safe, for example dangerous places, dangerous situations, the adults who will help, how to get help from others	8, 11, 14, 15
• Rules at home, at school and in the community	35, 38–41
• Respect and caring for people in the community, for example elderly people	38–40

Passport Learning Outcomes – Key Stage 1

Opportunities to enable pupils to:	Skills	Knowledge	Attitudes and values
1 Develop confidence and responsibility and make the most of their abilities	1 Recognise and name feelings, including those associated with changes, e.g. new family member. 2 Begin to manage feelings positively and effectively. 3 Ask for and give permission. 4 Recognise what they are good at from what others tell them. 5 Express positive qualities about themselves. 6 Respond with increasing confidence to new people and situations. 7 Set simple targets for themselves. 8 Perform simple tasks independently.	1 Know their personal likes and dislikes. 2 Understand ideas of good and bad, and right and wrong. 3 Know some of the things which can cause different emotions. 4 Know what they are good at. 5 Know that it is all right to make mistakes.	1 Believe in fairness for all. 2 Develop confidence when expressing opinions about things that matter to them. 3 Think about what responsibility means. 4 Recognise their uniqueness, feel good about themselves and be proud of their achievements. 5 Want to do well, and make the most of opportunities and talents. 6 Persevere and overcome difficulties.
2 Prepare to play an active role as citizens	1 Listen to the teacher and to a friend. 2 Hold the attention of a listener. 3 Ask simple questions of a range of adults. 4 Take part in discussions about matters relating to	1 Know the choices open to them, e.g. in food, games and activities. 2 Know the school and classroom rules and why they are necessary. 3 Know how to behave in different situations.	1 Be aware of their right to decide. 2 Think about what is important to them in making choices. 3 Think about their responsibilities to their friends, class, family.

their lives, e.g. the school environment, bullying.

5 Recognise and make safe choices based on right and wrong/good or bad.
6 Agree rules for the group/classroom.
7 Show some responsibility for self and others in and out of school, e.g. classroom, playground, school visits.
8 Observe surroundings and suggest how they might help to improve them.
9 Work together as a group or class on a project about a social or environmental issue.

4 Understand that other people, pets and plants have needs.
5 Know that all people have the same basic needs, and the difference between needs and wants.
6 Know the different groups to which they belong, e.g. family, friends, school.
7 Know the world including local services, e.g. library, leisure centre, museum, etc.
8 Know about the jobs of adults in the classroom, school and around them.
9 Know what improves and harms their local environment and how they can look after it.
10 Know about shops, services and advertising, and what they do for us; know that they have to pay for what they buy.

4 Care about people who have unmet needs.
5 Consider the value of being part of different groups and communities, e.g. a family and local community.
6 Appreciate and want to care for their environment: classroom, school grounds, local area.
7 Value natural resources and understand that they are limited.
8 Respect their own and other people's property, personal and public.
9 Show concern for the impact of their actions on others and the environment.
10 Want to participate, make a difference.
11 Think about how money can be spent other than on themselves.

3 Develop a healthy, safer lifestyle

1 Make simple choices, e.g. between foods, activities.
2 Maintain personal hygiene, e.g. washing, teeth cleaning, toilet routines.
3 Recognise potential risks to safety of self and others

1 Know what keeps them healthy: food, exercise.
2 Know that some people need drugs to live a normal life and that some drugs can prevent the development of disease, e.g. immunisation.

1 Be proud of their body, enjoy what it can do and treat it with respect.
2 Think about why it is important to know what they are eating.
3 Want to be healthy and clean.

from people, situations and in the environment.

4 Say 'no' when subject to pressure/something feels wrong.

5 Ask for help from adults.

6 Follow simple safety rules and instructions.

3 Understand the concept of growing from young to old and that they are growing and changing.

4 Know the correct names for the external parts of the body including the sexual parts.

5 Know what is safe to put into/onto the body and that all substances can be harmful if not used properly.

6 Know that all medicines are drugs but not all drugs are medicines.

7 Know places that are safe, where to get help and the people in their community who can help them.

8 Know the rules for keeping safe at home and at school, e.g. roads, fire, water, household substances, 'Stranger, Danger', knives, sun screens, medicines, tablets, and solvents.

9 Know when to keep a secret and when to tell.

10 Know that they have rights over their own bodies.

4 Think about why they need to take care and be safe in what they do.

5 Care about keeping themselves and others safe.

4 Develop good relationships and respect the differences between people

1 Voice differences of opinion sensitively and courteously; say 'sorry', 'thank you'.

2 Recognise ways in

1 Know that different types of family have common features and functions.

2 Know that there are similarities and differences

1 Consider the value of being a friend and having friends.

2 Be proud of who they are and understand that

which their own choices and behaviour affect others.

3   Co-operate with others in work and play; share; take turns.

4   Show respect by listening to what other people say.

5   Recognise worth in others, and say why someone is special to them.

6   Make new friends; cope with losing friends.

7   Help to care for pets and plants.

between people, gender, appearance, abilities, families, cultural backgrounds, etc.

3   Understand that boys and girls can both do the same tasks and enjoy the same things; but that stories and the television sometimes say that boys do this and girls do that.

4   Know that people have things in common but that every individual is unique.

5   Understand how to be a friend and that friendships can change.

6   Know the people who look after them and their different roles and responsibilities.

7   Know what bullying is and what to do if they experience or see bullying.

8   Understand that there is a difference between accidental and purposeful hurting.

difference does not mean better or worse.

3   Value other people's achievements.

4   Begin to accept everyone as an individual.

5   Respect other's needs, feelings and opinions.

6   Be willing to care for others.

7   Value the ways in which their family is special.

8   Think about what trust and reliability mean.

9   Think about why bullying is unacceptable.

QCA Scheme of Work for Citizenship

The QCA Scheme of Work for Citizenship is designed to offer schools flexibility in how they choose to address the aspects of the framework for PSHE and citizenship for Key Stage 1 that primarily involve citizenship. The following chart suggests the Blueprints units that are most relevant to each unit of the Scheme of Work. Four Blueprints units are suggested as resources for each Scheme of Work unit – two covering the relevant knowledge, skills and understanding, and two providing breadth of opportunity.

QCA Scheme of Work unit number and title	PSHE and Citizenship Framework objectives	Blueprints units
1 Taking part – developing skills of communication and participation	Knowledge, skills and understanding 1b, 1c, 1d, 2a, 2b, 2c, 2d	24 Please don't shout! 36 That hurts!
	Breadth of opportunity 5a 5c 5d 5g	26 Other people have feelings too 42 Put it to the vote
2 Choices	Knowledge, skills and understanding 1a, 1b, 2a, 2c, 3a, 4a	14 I take care of myself 35 What are rules for?
	Breadth of opportunity 5c, 5d, 5g	12 Secrets 32 The school community
3 Animals and us	Knowledge, skills and understanding 1b, 2a, 2b, 2e	27 Being a friend 41 Developing the language
	Breadth of opportunity 5a, 5c	34 The wider picture 39 We all need each other
4 People who help us – the local police	Knowledge, skills and understanding 1a, 1d, 2a, 2b, 2c, 2d, 2f, 3g, 4a, 4b, 4d	28 Helpful words and actions 37 Being truthful
	Breadth of opportunity 5c, 5e, 5h	11 Where do I feel safe? 30 Sharing and caring

	Knowledge, skills and understanding		
5 Living in a diverse world	Knowledge, skills and understanding 1b, 1c, 1d, 2a, 2b, 2e, 2f, 4a, 4b, 4c, 4d Breadth of opportunity 5a, 5b, 5c, 5e, 5g	31 Looking around us 40 Being together 23 Finding the words 25 A rainbow of feelings
6 Developing our school grounds	Knowledge, skills and understanding 1a, 1b, 1e, 2a, 2d, 2e, 2h, 2i, 4a, 4b Breadth of opportunity 5a, 5c, 5d, 5e, 5h	33 The world is precious 38 This is where I live 3 Look what I can do now 18 Keeping fit and well

Looking good and keeping well

1 Staying healthy

Aims

- To begin to raise awareness of the responsibility we all have to keep ourselves healthy.
- To begin to consider that the ways we look after/do not look after our bodies and emotions can influence how healthy we are.

Teaching points

This activity is recommended as an introductory lesson for each year group of children.

It is important to explore with the children the many different meanings the terms 'healthy' and 'not so healthy' have to different people and to raise the issue that it is not just about being free from illness or disease.

Be sensitive to the fact that there may be children with relatives/friends who are ill, and make it clear that if someone wears glasses, wears a hearing aid, is in a wheelchair … it does not mean that he/she is not healthy. Please also note the deliberate use of 'healthy' and 'not so healthy' as opposed to 'healthy' and 'unhealthy', which can give a more negative and final message to children.

Instructions

1 Distribute a sheet of A4 paper to each child. Invite the children to draw an outline of a person (a gingerbread person or a stick person).

2 Now ask them to draw and/or write around the person all the things they can think of that will help to make and keep the person healthy. (Encourage them to put down as many ideas as they can and not worry too much about whether they are right or wrong.)

3 Review the ideas by drawing an outline of a person on the board and writing the children's contributions around the person.

4 Discuss with the children why they think those things help to keep a person healthy and add any important ones which have been missed (for example, caring for each other, sharing our feelings, resting, praying, having fun …).

5 Ask the children to draw another outline of a person on the other side of their piece of paper and repeat Instructions 2–4 for a not so healthy person.

6 Invite the children to complete Activity Sheet 1 as a summary and reinforcement of the discussion. Explain that the pictures at the top of the sheet show some things that can help to keep you healthy and some that can help to make you not so healthy. Point out that some things are always not so healthy (cigarettes) but others (chips/chocolate) only if out of balance with healthy food. Ask them to copy the pictures around either the 'healthy person' or the 'not so healthy' person accordingly.

Resources

1 sheet of A4 paper for each child
Pencils/pens
Photocopies of Activity Sheet 1

Extension activities

Cut out two large outlines of a person (you can draw round a child if it is easier!) and attach them to a classroom wall. Invite the children to bring in pictures from magazines or to draw their own pictures of what helps to keep a person healthy/not so healthy. Attach these to the outlines to make a 'person collage'.

My Body Your Body by Mick Manning and Brita Granstrom, Wonderwise Book, Franklin Watts.
ISBN 0-7496-2898-7

Keeping healthy

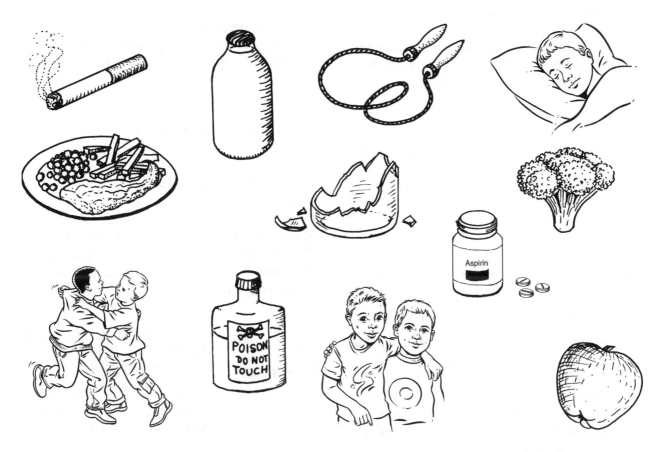

A healthy person　　　　　　**A not so healthy person**

Growing and changing

2 Shapes and sizes

Aims
- To enable children to acknowledge and accept that people are all different shapes and sizes.
- To enable children to begin to understand their own body shapes and sizes and how their bodies will grow and change.

Teaching points
Children may need to be encouraged to be sensitive to other children's feelings about their shape and size and the language used to describe them.

Instructions
1 Draw the following shapes on the board:

    large square   small square
    large circle   small circle

2 Discuss with the children what is similar about the shapes and what is different about them. (Reinforce the fact that the two shapes with straight sides are both squares although they are different sizes, and the two round shapes are both circles although they are different sizes.)

3 Draw up a list of words with the children that describe how people look and what makes them different.

    tall   thin
    eye colour   hair colour   long hair
    not so thin   skin colour   small
    can walk   moves in a wheelchair

4 Ask the children which of these might change as people grow older, and put a circle around the identified words.

5 Invite them to complete Activity Sheet 2 instructing them to draw two people who are very different in shape and size and to label all the differences that they can think of.

Resources
Photocopies of Activity Sheet 2

Extension activities
Invite each child to draw around his/her hand (or they can work in pairs and draw around each other's hand) and then cut it out. Ask the children to write their names on the drawings of their hands and then assemble them to make a 'hand collage of Our Class'.

All Kinds of People by Emma Damon, Tango Books.
ISBN 1-85707-067-4

Nancy No-Size by Mary Hoffman, Mammoth Books.
ISBN 0-7497-0090-4

Growing and changing

Draw a picture of two people who are a different size and shape to each other. Label all the differences that you can think of.

We are all different shapes and sizes. We are all special.

Growing and changing

3 Look what I can do now

Aims
- To raise awareness that babies and children grow and change as a normal part of life.
- To help children to reflect on their own growth and development.

Teaching points
We all grow and change from birth until we become adults. As we grow older our bodies change and we are able to do more and more things for ourselves.

Instructions
1 Talk with the children about babies. Who has a baby living at home? What are the kind of things that we have to do for babies because they cannot do them for themselves?

2 Make a list with the children of all the things they could not do when they were babies that they can do now.

3 Ask them how they know that they have grown. The following questions may be useful to raise some points:

- What can you reach now that you could not reach one year ago?
- How do you know your feet have grown?
- Which parts of your body do you cut when they grow?
- Does everyone here have the same teeth they had as babies?

4 Invite the children to complete Activity Sheet 3 by writing around the baby all the things with which it needs help. They should then draw a picture of themselves and, on the lines at the bottom of the sheet, write all the things they can think of that they can do now but could not do as a baby.

5 Finally, discuss with the children the kind of things that they cannot do yet but will be able to do in the near future.

You could close the session by asking every child to tell you one thing he/she is really looking forward to being able to do but cannot do yet.

Resources
Photocopies of Activity Sheet 3

Extension activities
This is a good opportunity to invite a parent with a young baby into the class to talk about the ways in which the baby has to be cared for.

Once There Were Giants by Martin Waddell and Penny Dale, Walker Books.
ISBN 0-7445-1791-5
This tells the story of a baby changing, growing and developing.

Nearly But Not Quite by Paul Rogers and John Prater, The Bodley Head Children's Books.
ISBN 0-370-32423-4

Look what I can do now

Write around the picture of the
baby all the things you can think
of that a baby needs help with.

This is me now.
Draw a picture of yourself in
the box below.

Now I can:

....

....

....

....

....

....

Blueprints PSHE and Citizenship Key Stage 1 © Judy Hunter and Sheila Phillips, Nelson Thornes Ltd, 2002

Growing and changing

4 Where do we grow from?

Aims
- To understand how some animals grow and develop.
- To understand where human babies grow from.

Teaching points
It takes different lengths of time for different baby animals to grow and develop before they are ready to be born. It takes nine months for a human baby to grow and develop before it is big and strong enough to be born. Sometimes babies are born before nine months and then they may need extra help from doctors and nurses to make them strong.

Some animals lay their eggs (for example birds) but other animals and mammals make eggs that develop inside their bodies and the offspring are born as babies.

Instructions
1   Discuss with the children where some animals come from – dogs, cats, horses, hamsters, guinea pigs, sheep ... (perhaps some of the children may have seen an animal being born).

2   Does anyone know what is a little bit different about how frogs grow and develop?

3   Does anyone know how butterflies grow and develop?

You may find it useful to read the story of *The Very Hungry Caterpillar* by Eric Carle, Puffin Books.
ISBN 0-14-050087-1

4   What about human babies – what do they grow from? (They grow from an egg. An egg is the beginning of a baby.)

Where do they grow? (They grow inside their mothers from a very tiny egg.)

5   Invite the children to complete Activity Sheet 4 which asks them to match each baby with the correct mother and to complete the sentence at the bottom of the sheet.

Resources
Photocopies of Activity Sheet 4

Extension activities
Contact your local health centre and ask if a midwife could come in to talk to the children about how he/she helps mothers prepare for their babies being born and what help a baby needs just after it has been born.

You may also like to arrange a visit to a farm if you have one nearby that caters for visits by schoolchildren.

The World Is Full Of Babies by Mick Manning and Brita Granstrom, Wonderwise Books, Franklin Watts.
ISBN 0-7496-2752-2

Where do we grow from?

Draw a line from the baby to the correct mother.

A human baby grows inside its m_____ _____ from a tiny e____ ___

and takes n____ _____ months to grow big and strong enough to be born.

Growing and changing

5 What helps me to grow?

Aims

- To understand the importance of keeping as healthy as possible to help our bodies grow and develop.
- To understand that other people help us to keep healthy and we can help ourselves as well.

Teaching points

This activity also links with citizenship issues of interdependence and members of a community supporting each other.

Be sensitive to the fact that some children may come from homes where they do not have the opportunity to take part in many activities or eat a varied and balanced diet. It is important that children are not given the message that the food they eat at home is 'unhealthy' or that they are not being helped to grow and develop as healthily as possible. Place the emphasis on what they can do to help themselves now they are getting older.

Instructions

1 Gather a list from the children of all the people they might see in school (roles not individuals).

> teachers   school nurse   friends
> lunchtime staff   parent helpers
> school doctor   lollipop person

2 How do these people help us?

How can we help them?

What will we do for ourselves as we grow older that they do for us now?

3 Gather a list from the children of all the people they might see at home (roles not individuals).

> parents/carers   window cleaner
> brother/sister   postperson   doctor
> milkman   baby-sitter   grandparents

4 How do these people help us?

How can we help them?

What will we do for ourselves as we grow older that they do for us now?

5 Discuss with the children what 'things' help us to grow and develop, rather than people who help us grow and develop, and invite them to complete Activity Sheet 5 by writing in the words for these things as though they were being poured out of the watering can. (Children can draw in pictures if they or you prefer instead of writing the words.)

Resources

Photocopies of Activity Sheet 5

Extension activities

If you keep a class pet, you can ask the children to keep a journal of all the people who help to look after the pet and what things the pet needs to help it grow. If not, perhaps the children can work in small groups in which at least one of them has a pet, and together they can write a similar journal.

The children can look at how plants grow and keep a record of how they have to care for them, how much they grow, and so on.

I'm Falling To Bits by Ted Arnold, MacDonald Young Books.
ISBN 0-7500-2481-X

Growing Pains by Jenny Stow, Frances Lincoln Ltd.
ISBN 0-7112-0955-3

What helps me to grow?

Things that help me to grow

Exercising   Sleeping

Growing and changing

6 There are names for everything

Aims
- To know the correct names for the external parts of the body, including the sexual parts.
- To know that the bodies of males and females have similarities and differences.

Teaching points
It is helpful to have the parents' involvement and an excellent way to to do this is to ask them to teach their children the biological names for the outer sexual body parts before they start school. At the same time parents can also be asked to ensure their children know how to ask to go to the toilet, in language that can be clearly understood, and how to manage for themselves when going to the toilet. Most parents will understand the benefit of children having a common language. It might be helpful to prepare a parents' information sheet for them. You will still need to teach the names of the sexual body parts in class to children who have not been taught them at home.

Clarity of language is important. Adults need to make sure they understand what children are saying to them and that children understand what adults are saying to them.

Instructions
1   Draw the outline of a person on the board (genderless). Invite the children to tell you the names of different parts of the body and write these against the outline of the person.

2   Ask the children whether the person is a boy or a girl. How do we know/not know?

3   Explain to the children that some parts of the bodies of boys and girls are different, and that, like the other parts of our bodies, those parts have names too.

4   Draw the outline of another person on the board and explain to the children that this outline is a girl and the other outline is a boy.

5   Complete the words for the body parts of the boy by writing 'penis' and 'testicles'. Explain that all the words for the body parts of the girl are exactly the same, except that a girl does not have a penis or testicles. Girls have 'breasts' and a 'vagina'. (Write these words on the second outline.)

6   Reassure the children that everyone probably has different words they use to describe these parts of the body and accept the language they may give you. (It is best not to use any other words yourself.) The language we use at home may be different and that is fine, but in school it is important for everybody to use the names written on the board.

7   Invite the children to complete Activity Sheet 6 by copying the names of the body parts from the board.

Resources
Photocopies of Activity Sheet 6

Extension activities
Draw the outlines of a boy and a girl on very large pieces of paper. Write the names of body parts on stickers and divide the class into two groups to see how quickly they can place the stickers over the correct part of the body.

6
Activity
Sheet

There are names for everything

This is a picture of a boy.
Write in all the names of the
body parts.

This is a picture of a girl.
Write in all the names of the
body parts.

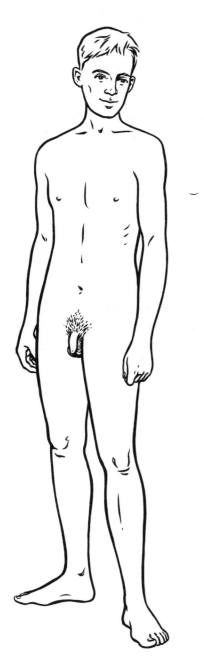

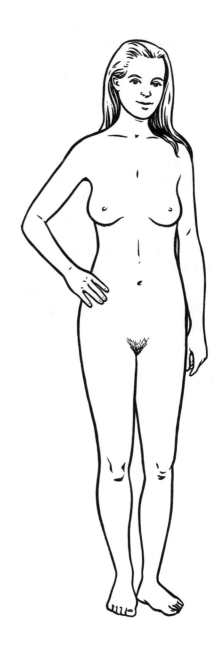

This is a picture of a boy.
I know he is a boy because he
has a penis and testicles.

This is a picture of a girl.
I know she is a girl because
she has a vagina and breasts.

Medicines and drugs

7 Sometimes I need medicines

Aims

● To develop an understanding of different kinds of medicines that are used to help people who are ill.

● To develop an emotional language associated with feeling well and feeling ill.

Teaching points

Be aware that some children may have concerns about family members who are ill. Children will need support to extend their emotional vocabulary beyond 'well' and 'ill' and the development of an emotional language is an integral part of PSHE education.

Instructions

1   Ask the children to think of a time when they felt ill. How did they know they were ill? (Spots, being hot, being cold, runny nose, cough, sore throat, pain ...) What words can they think of to describe how we might feel when we are not very well?

Gather these words from the children (you may like to keep them or copy them later to put on the wall as a reminder of the language).

sad   worried   sick   fed up   tired
poorly   unhappy   cosy   cared for

2   Invite the children to complete the first part of Activity Sheet 7 by drawing a picture of themselves when they were not well and to write around the picture any words to describe how they felt.

3   Now ask the children to think about when they feel well. Ask them to think of some words that describe how we might feel when

we are well. Gather these words from the children, which again you might like to keep.

fit   healthy   full of energy   happy
OK   brilliant   wonderful

4   Invite the children to complete the second part of Activity Sheet 7 by drawing a picture of themselves when they are well and to write around the picture any words to describe how they feel.

5   Now ask the children to think of all the different ways people can be given medicine to help them feel better (injections, medicine on a spoon, drops, asthma sprays, creams and ointments). Remind them that safe medicine can be unsafe if too much is taken, or it is taken by the wrong person. Ask them to complete the third part of Activity Sheet 7.

Resources

Photocopies of Activity Sheet 7

Extension activities

This is an ideal opportunity to explain why some children need to take medicines such as asthma sprays and how this helps them. The children who regularly take medicines may also have some questions that they have never been encouraged to ask, so give them time to discuss and explore any concerns or questions they may have. They might like to say what help they feel they need (if any) from the other children to help them with their illness.

 Six Dinner Sid by Inga Moore, Simon & Schuster Books for Young Readers. ISBN 0671796135

Name .... Date ....

Sometimes I need medicines

1 This is me when I am ill.

2 This is me when I am well.

3 Here are some different kinds of medicine that can help me to feel better when I am ill.

....

....

....

....

....

Write the correct word next to each picture.

| Spray | Medicine | Cream | Drops | Injection |

Medicines and drugs

8 Who should I take medicines from?

Aims
- To develop an understanding of who is authorised to give them medicines.
- To develop an understanding of how medicines should be looked after.

Teaching points
Be aware that not all families will store medicines as safely as possible and be careful not to criticise children's homes or frighten the children about medicines they may see at home. Some children may need reassurance if they have relatives who regularly take medication and they may need some help to understand why this is the case. Encourage them to talk at home about the work they have been doing in school so that parents/carers have an opportunity to reinforce the messages you are trying to convey.

Remember it is important to model the safe handling of medicines in school so that children see that what you do is consistent with what you are saying. Health messages need to be 'lived'!

Instructions
1. Ask the children to think about when they have been ill and needed some medicine – who gave it to them? How did they know it was safe to take the medicine from that person?

2. Make a list of the people from whom it is safe to take medicines and discuss in each case how they know it is safe to take medicines from that person.

3. Ask the children where medicines come from. (Doctor, chemist, shop ...) Which are the best places for keeping medicines safely? (Medicine cupboard, drawer, handbag ...)

4. Invite the children to complete Activity Sheet 8 by putting a tick or a cross in the box next to each picture depending on whether they think the medicine is being stored safely or not.

5. Draw up some simple rules with the children about storing and taking medicines, for example:

   - Remember medicines can be dangerous if they are not taken safely.
   - Take medicines only from someone who it is safe to take them from.
   - Keep all medicines in a safe place.
   - If someone who is not a safe person asks you to touch or taste a medicine say 'No' and tell an adult.

Resources
Photocopies of Activity Sheet 8

Extension activities
The children can copy the rules either by hand or on a computer and display them around other areas of the school to reinforce messages for other children (and adults). Help the children to practise ways of saying 'No' in different situations in which someone is trying to persuade them to touch or taste something that might not be safe or to do something that might not be safe.

 Nice or Nasty? Learning about Drugs and Your Health by Claire Llewellyn, Wayland Publishers Ltd.
ISBN 0-7502-2332-4

Who should I take medicines from?

Put a tick (✔) in the box if you think the medicine is being stored safely.
Put a cross (✘) in the box if you think the medicine is not being stored safely.

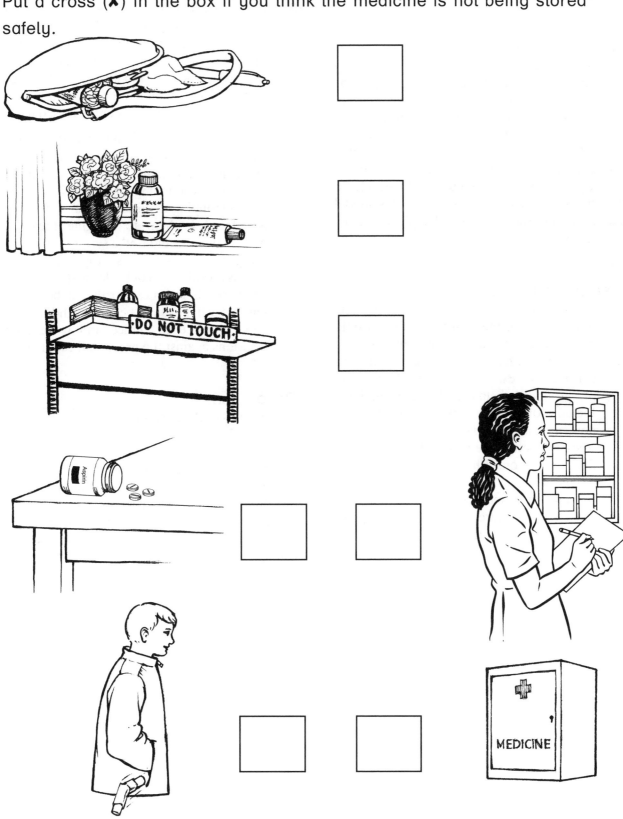

Medicines and drugs

9 Should I put it in my mouth?

Aims

● To develop an understanding of what can be dangerous to taste or put on our skin.

● To reinforce awareness of how to keep as safe as possible.

Teaching points

Children need to understand that just tasting something, even without swallowing it, can be dangerous. There are also some things that are dangerous if put on our skin. Children cannot be supervised all the time so they need to understand that they also have a responsibility for keeping themselves safe. It can be useful to develop the model of **stop**, **think**, **decide** in health education and you can put this model against a set of traffic lights and apply it to many different situations.

Instructions

1 Draw up a list with the children of as many different things they can think of that would not be safe to put in their mouths. Give the children different environments to consider, for example in the kitchen, in the playground, to help broaden their thinking. Include some ideas of your own if they do not suggest things such as berries from trees, cigarettes, medicines that they might find, and so on. When the list is complete discuss why each one would not be safe to put into their mouths. (Alternatively, you can ask the children to work in groups to draw up lists and then bring all the ideas together.)

2 Now ask the children what it would not be safe to touch or put on their skin (broken glass, a syringe, someone else's cream/ointment, cleaning fluids, very strong glue, something sharp, something hot), and again discuss why each one might not be safe.

3 Invite the children to complete Activity Sheet 9 by drawing or writing the words for things that are not safe to go into the mouth under the closed mouth, and things that are safe to go into the mouth under the open mouth. They should draw or write things they should not touch under the closed hand.

4 Draw a set of traffic lights and ask the children what the colours red, amber and green mean. Explain that they can make decisions by thinking of traffic lights and always stopping to think whether something is safe. Ask them to imagine they are playing outside and find a syringe – the first thing they must do is stop and think. Discuss what they could do next and write all these choices next to the amber light. Discuss what would be good and not so good about each choice and write their decisions against the green and red lights.

Resources

Photocopies of Activity Sheet 9

Extension activities

Encourage the children to begin thinking about possible safety hazards in school and to notice them during the rest of the day/week. You can then discuss these in class. If you have a school council, the class representative can take one of the issues forward to the council for discussion to see how it could be made safer.

Name .... Date ....

Should I put it in my mouth?

Draw or write words under the picture of the **closed mouth** to describe the things that it is **not safe** to put into our mouths.

Draw or write words under the picture of the **open mouth** to describe the things that it is **safe** to put into our mouths.

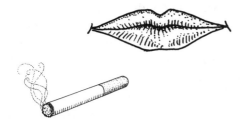

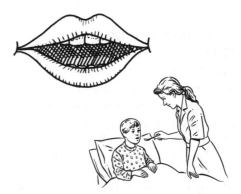

Draw or write words to describe all the things you can think of that it **would not be safe to touch** under the picture of the **closed hand**.

Medicines and drugs

10 Germbusters!

Aims
- To develop an understanding of what germs are and how they can spread.
- To develop an understanding of how we can help our bodies to fight germs.
- To develop an understanding of how medicines can be used to make our immune system stronger.

Teaching points
Helping children to understand something about their immune system is laying the foundation for good HIV/AIDS education in later years. AIDS can be explained as a virus which tries to break down their germbuster system. In the early years this is often as much information as children want and it answers their questions honestly.

Ideally this lesson should be used as preparation for vaccination programmes in schools. Very often, little attention is given to preparing the children at all and yet this is health education in action! The school nurse could also take part in this lesson and answer any questions the children have.

Instructions
1 Ask the children: Who knows anything about germs? Can you see germs? How are germs spread?

2 How can we help to stop germs spreading? (Using a handkerchief when sneezing, washing our hands after we have been to the toilet, covering food ...)

3 Explain that there are different types of germs: some germs are called bacteria and some germs are called viruses – chickenpox, for example, is a virus. If we become ill because germs have entered our bodies, we have something in our bodies which helps to fight the germs – white cells in our blood. (Blood is made up of water, red blood cells, white blood cells and platelets.) We are going to call this our germbuster system.

4 Explain to the children that white blood cells can be seen only under a microscope, but ask them to imagine they can see one – it is a germbuster and is ready to fight germs that get into the body. Ask them to draw it at the top of Activity Sheet 10.

5 Invite them to share their drawings with the class. Now ask them what they think could help to make their germbuster system even stronger. What might help if our germbuster system was still not strong enough?

6 Review with the children the different ways we can be given medicine and, if this lesson is leading up to a vaccination programme, explain that they will be getting some medicine in the form of an injection which will help to make their germbuster system stronger. Discuss with the children any fears or concerns they have.

7 Invite the children to complete the second part of Activity Sheet 10 by drawing or writing all the things that can help to make their germbuster system even stronger.

N.B. Please be sensitive to the fact that some parents may not agree with vaccination. If this is the case, it is important to explain that some people feel that if we take care of our bodies, they will be strong and will grow their own germbusters.

Resources
Photocopies of Activity Sheet 10

Extension activities
The children can draw up some simple rules for helping to fight germs in school.

If a microscope is available, children can learn how microscopes enable us to see things that we would not normally be able to see with just our eyes.

 I Know How We Fight Germs (Sam's Science Series) by Kate Rowan, Walker Books. ISBN 0-7445-7222-3

Germbusters!

Draw below what you think a germbuster might look like.

Draw or write below all the things you can think of that can help to make your germbuster system stronger.

Keeping safer

11 Where do I feel safe?

Aims
- To raise awareness of the need for children to take some responsibility for keeping safe.
- To develop an emotional language in relation to feeling safe and unsafe.
- To enable children to consider how they can contribute to making their school a safe place to be.

Teaching points
Whilst the intention is not to frighten children, it is important that they begin to understand that they have some responsibility to do their best to keep themselves safe and that they can also help others to feel safe by their behaviour and the care they show towards them. If children display any form of bullying behaviour or aggression towards others, they need to be gently encouraged to understand that they can learn to control and change their behaviour – this also forms part of the citizenship curriculum.

The extent to which children will feel free to talk about their emotions and what helps them to feel safe or unsafe will largely depend on how safe and secure they feel in the classroom. It is essential, therefore, to consider how safe the classroom is as a learning environment. For example, is it safe to make mistakes without fear of being humiliated or ridiculed?

Be sensitive to the fact that, for some children, their own homes may not feel like safe places to be.

Instructions
1   Explain to the children that they are going to be considering ways of keeping themselves safe and ask them to complete the first part of Activity Sheet 11, drawing a special place where they feel safe.

2   Invite them to say something about what they have drawn and why these feel like safe places to be.

3   Gather words with the children to describe what makes a place safe and what it feels like to be there.

4   Now ask the children to think about places where it does not feel so safe. What might these places be and why might they not be safe?

5   Gather words with the children to describe what makes a place unsafe and what it feels like to be there.

6   Which places should they not go to and which situations should they not get into because it might not be safe?

    What should they do if someone tries to encourage them to go somewhere that is not safe or to do something that is not safe?

7   Discuss with the children whether school feels like a safe place to be. Which places in school feel safe and which feel less safe, and why is this?

8   With the children, draw up some simple rules for making school as safe a place as possible, particularly from the point of view of caring for each other.

9   Ask the children to copy the rules on the second part of Activity Sheet 11.

Resources
Photocopies of Activity Sheet 11

Extension activities
You may be able to bring in a visitor to discuss road safety with the children. You could try contacting your local police school liaison officer. This may also be a good opportunity to invite the local lollipop person into school to meet the children.

You're Safe Now Waterdog by Richard Edwards, Orion Children's Books.
ISBN 1-85881-279-8

Name .... Date ....

II
Activity Sheet

Where do I feel safe?

Draw below a special place where you feel safe.

My special place is .... and I feel safe there because

....

Our rules for making this school a safe place to be are:

Blueprints PSHE and Citizenship Key Stage 1 © Judy Hunter and Sheila Phillips, Nelson Thornes Ltd, 2002

Keeping safer

12 Secrets

Aims

- To explore the issue of 'nice touches' and 'not so nice' touches.
- To raise awareness in children that they do not have to be touched in ways that they may not want to be touched.
- To develop an understanding of what secrets it is important not to keep.

Teaching points

Although this is a sensitive issue, it is an important one to raise. Make sure you are fully up-to-date with the school child protection procedures and be alert to any concerns you may have about how children respond to this topic and any disclosures they may make.

Instructions

1   Explain to the children that babies do not have a choice about being cuddled and touched but we do. Being cuddled and touched can be nice but only when we want to be cuddled and touched and by people by whom we want to be cuddled.

2   With the children, gather two boxes of words to describe 'nice touches' and 'not so nice touches':

Nice touches	Not so nice touches	
shaking hands	punching	kicking
tickling	pushing	nipping
holding hands	tickling	slapping
kissing	kissing	cuddling
cuddling		

3   Ask the children what they can do if someone touches them and they do not want them to. Who could they tell – at home, in school, out playing?

4   Discuss with the children: Has anyone ever been asked to keep a secret? Have you ever asked anyone to keep a secret? It's nice sometimes to share secrets with friends but some things should not be kept secret. Which things do you think are OK to keep secret and which things are not OK to keep secret?

Make sure the children understand that if someone touches them and asks them to keep it a secret, it is not OK to keep that secret and it is important to tell someone.

5   Ask the children to complete Activity Sheet 12 by drawing people they could tell if someone touched them and they did not want to be touched by them, and making a list of secrets that are OK to keep and secrets that are not OK to keep.

Resources

Photocopies of Activity Sheet 12

Extension activities

Ask the children to be aware of their behaviour towards each other in the playground and not to touch anyone in ways that they do not want to be touched.

Agree with the children a signal or a phrase that they can use when they really need to be listened to because they have something important to share.

Extend the theme of 'touches' to language development by asking the children to describe how different materials and textures feel. For example, make a 'Joseph Jacket' to go on the classroom wall made up of all different materials (satin, velvet, sandpaper, sequins, cotton wool, tissue paper ...). Invite the children to feel the different textures and generate words to describe how they feel.

Not Now Bernard by David McKee, Random Century Children's Books.
ISBN 0-09-924050-5

Uncle Willy's Tickles by Marcie Aboff, Magination Press.
ISBN 0-945354-67-3

Name .... Date ....

Secrets

If someone touches me and I do not want them to, I can tell ...

Draw the people who you can tell and say who they are.

Now write down below the
secrets you think are OK to keep
and the secrets you think are
not OK to keep.

Secrets that are OK to keep   **Secrets that are not OK to keep**

Blueprints PSHE and Citizenship Key Stage 1 © Judy Hunter and Sheila Phillips, Nelson Thornes Ltd, 2002

Keeping safer

13 Enjoying the sunshine

Aims
- To raise awareness of sun safety issues.
- To enable children to play a role in keeping themselves safe in the sun.

Teaching points
Whilst sun safety might not spring readily to mind as something that we need to educate even very young children about, it is something that is causing increasing concern to health professionals. This is a topic that really does need the messages to be put into practice in school: Are children encouraged to wear hats at playtimes and lunchtimes in sunny weather? How are children (and adults) encouraged to protect their skin on sports days? Your local Health Promotion Department will be able to provide you with leaflets and information that can be distributed to parents so that you can encourage them to work with you to reinforce messages about keeping safe in the sun.

Instructions
1 Ask the children to imagine a very cold, crisp day and that they want to go out and play in the snow. How would they make sure they kept warm and dry? Gather their ideas and discuss how all of these things help them to take care of their bodies in cold weather.

2 Now ask them to imagine a very warm, sunny day and that they want to go out and play, perhaps on the beach or in the park. How would they make sure they kept cool and safe in the sun? Gather their ideas and discuss how all of these things help them to take care of their bodies in sunny weather. Explain how the sun can cause damage to our skin and that we should only go out in it for short periods of time. It is best to keep in the shade when we can.

3 Ask the children to complete Activity Sheet 13 by looking at the pictures at the top of the page and deciding what they would pack in their bags if they were going out to the beach or the park on a sunny day. Ask them to draw and write the word for each item on the bag.

Resources
Photocopies of Activity Sheet 13

Extension activities
The children can write a letter to their parents/carers explaining what they need to bring to school to protect themselves when playing in the sun.

This is an opportunity to discuss why some people have black skin, some people have brown skin and some people have white skin.

Using the theme of warm/sunny and cold/wet, build the children's emotional literacy by generating a list of things that help them to feel warm/sunny and a list of things that help them to feel cold/wet. When is this classroom warm and sunny?

Name .... Date ....

Enjoying the sunshine

sunglasses

scarf

sun hat

gloves

woolly hat

sun cream

T-shirt

bottle of water

hot water bottle

swimming trunks

towel

shorts

swimsuit

wellington boots

Draw and write on the bag what you are going to take with you to the beach or the park on a hot day.

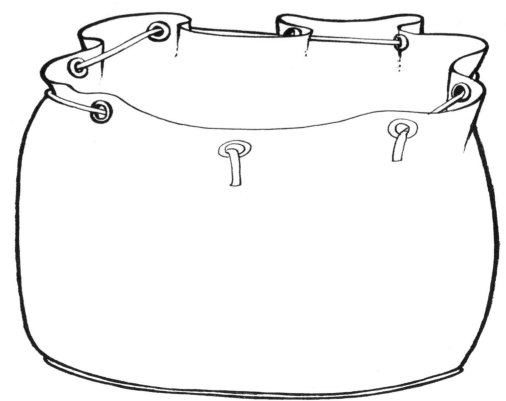

Keeping safer

14 I take care of myself

Aims
- To develop an understanding in children of the need to be responsible for taking care of themselves.
- To consider different situations that might be unsafe and explore possible options for dealing with them.

Teaching points
It is sometimes difficult for children to imagine how some situations could present a threat to their personal safety – this is all part of the skill of being able to look ahead and think about the possible consequences of their actions. We need to help children to develop the skill of looking beyond their immediate needs and feelings and to raise their awareness of how vulnerable they can be, without frightening or shocking them. Remember that through literature we can place children in situations which they would not normally be able to enter. Through the characters children can experience feelings, consider options and flex their decision-making muscles without coming to any harm. Therefore, maximise opportunities that arise through literature and poetry to continue this theme.

Instructions
1   Ask the children to think of something that is very special to them and invite them to share it with the class and to say how they take care of it.

2   Generate a list of these special things and ask the children what is special about each one of them. Now ask them to consider how they look after themselves and to share this with the class.

3   Take the following scenarios (or as many as you choose) and discuss each one with the children, listing as many different ways as possible for keeping safe in each different scenario: 'Keeping safe on the road', 'Keeping safe in the playground', 'Keeping safe in the sun', and so on. (If you prefer you can ask the children to work in small groups and role-play keeping safe in the different situations while the other children watch and try to guess what they are demonstrating.)

4   Discuss with the children how they could contact the police, ambulance service, fire service if they, or someone else, was in real danger; for example, if they were at home with someone who was taken very ill and there was no one else in.

- What telephone number would you dial?
- What would you say?
- Would you be able to clearly tell the person on the phone your name and address?

5   Invite the children to complete Activity Sheet 14, instructing them to write the details asked for to make up their own 'keeping safer' invitation card, which they can then cut out.

Resources
Scissors
Photocopies of Activity Sheet 14

Extension activities
Follow up this lesson with the danger of making hoax phone calls to the emergency services. Your local fire service may be able to support you and also deliver a home safety/fire safety session with the children.

The children can devise a series of keeping safer posters basing them on the scenarios in Instruction 3 above.

 You Are Very Special by Su Box, Lion Books.
ISBN 0-7459-3348-3

I take care of myself

Complete the invitation and then cut it out.

KEEPING SAFER INVITATION

You are invited to take care of yourself and keep safe because you are a very special person.

My name is

....

I live at

....

....

If I got lost I would tell

....

If someone I did not trust said 'Come with me' or 'Get in my car' I would

....

If I had to telephone the police or the fire service or the ambulance service I would dial

☎ ....

Keeping safer

15 It depends on you

Aims
- To raise awareness that we are surrounded by everyday objects that can be dangerous if misused and safe if handled with care.
- To generate discussion with the children about ways of keeping themselves safe.

Teaching points
Children need to know enough to keep themselves as safe as possible. We cannot be with children every minute of every day and even everyday objects can be unsafe if we do not take care. Objects that we might consider to be highly dangerous, on the other hand, can be perfectly safe if used properly. For example, children might immediately say that a syringe is dangerous, but we need syringes for medical care and they are perfectly safe when used properly and by the right people.

Keeping safer is part of the skill of developing responsibility and independence.

Instructions
1   Activity Sheet 15 is used as a stimulus for discussion. Discuss each picture with the whole class or, alternatively, ask the children to work in small groups and then share their ideas. For each picture, ask them to decide when it could be unsafe, i.e. how might it be dangerous, and when it could be safe, i.e. what care would need to be taken.

2   Ask the children to notice what hazards there may be around them and to notice how even simple things can cause harm if we misuse them. Review their ideas in the next lesson.

Resources
Photocopies of Activity Sheet 15

Extension activities
Follow up on specific aspects of keeping safer, for example fire safety. Your local fire station may be able to arrange for someone from their service to talk to the children.
Fireworks safety (often the Environmental Health Department will help) or water safety are other specific aspects you could explore.

Name.. Date ....

It depends on you

Look at each picture and decide when these things or situations could be safe and when they could be unsafe.

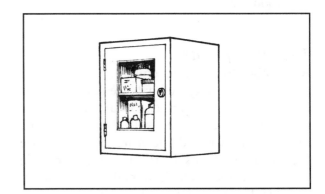

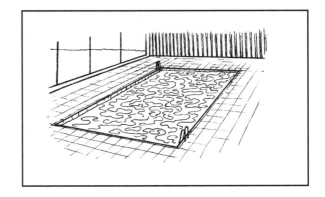

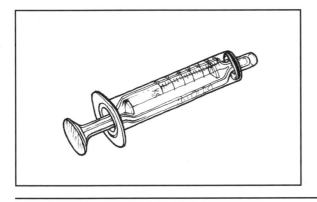

Eating and exercise

16 My body needs energy

Aims

- To develop an understanding that food is fuel which the body converts into energy.
- To develop an understanding that some foods provide more energy than others and to raise awareness of what some of these foods are.

Teaching points

Remember that some children may not be provided with a very well-balanced diet at home. It is important not to criticise what they are given at home or to leave them with the message that their parents/carers do not care enough to give them healthier foods. It is best to concentrate on the food choices children make in school if possible. Use the language 'foods to eat more of' and 'foods to eat less of'. Always avoid talking about 'good' and 'bad' foods or 'healthy' and 'unhealthy' foods and help the children to understand that no food is bad for you, it is just that we need more of some foods than others to keep healthy.

Instructions

1   Ask the children what we put into cars to make them go.

    What happens when a car runs out of fuel?

2   What do we put into our bodies to make them work? Explain that food is converted into energy and ask the children which activities use a lot of energy and which activities do not use so much energy.

3   Discuss with the children what kinds of food give us plenty of energy. Introduce the words 'fats', 'proteins', 'carbohydrates', 'vitamins' and 'minerals', and explain that we need all of these to keep as healthy as we can but that we need more of some foods than others.

4   Ask the children to give you some examples of foods and write these on the board.

Explain that you are now going to write these foods against a set of traffic lights (draw the traffic lights). **Red** means foods we should eat just a little of, **Amber** means foods we need some of every day and **Green** means foods we can eat a lot of. Here is a guide:

Red – pizza, burgers, chips, roast potatoes, sausages, butter, cream, fizzy pop, cakes, chocolate biscuits, Yorkshire puddings, sweets, chocolate, beef, fish in batter
Amber – bread, pasta, potatoes, cheese, yoghurts, eggs, milk, pork, chicken, cereals
Green – fruit, vegetables, fruit juices, drinks with no added sugar, fish, slices of ham or chicken, water

5   Invite the children to complete Activity Sheet 16 by joining each food to red, amber or green, depending on where they think they should go.

Resources

Coloured pens (red, yellow, green) for every child
Photocopies of Activity Sheet 16

Extension activities

Work with your school meals service to develop the traffic light system for school lunches by displaying red, amber or green against meal choices to help the children to choose a balanced meal. If this can be displayed at child's eye level with pictures of 'Today's choices' the children can make their choice while in the queue.

Cut out pictures of different types of foods and make a food pyramid to display in the classroom with green foods on the bottom, amber foods in the middle and red foods at the top.

 Eat Up Gemma by Sarah Hayes, Walker Books Ltd. ISBN 0-7445-1328-6

My body needs energy

Look at the different foods. Decide whether you think they are **Red** foods (foods we should only eat a little of), **Amber** foods (foods we need some of every day) or **Green** foods (foods we can eat a lot of). Draw a line in the correct colour from each food to the correct light.

Eating and exercise

17 Choosing lunch

Aims
- To develop an understanding of the notion of balanced meals.
- To raise awareness that children can take some responsibility for what they choose to eat.

Teaching points
It is helpful to take the opportunity to link this with cultural education and discuss the different foods that people from different cultures eat. You may find that your school meals service is able to arrange some school meals with different themes. If not, provide a selection of foods so that the children can have a food tasting session. Parents may also become involved.

Beware in case you have any children with food allergies – check carefully before allowing them to sample any foods. You can discuss with the children what food allergies are and why some people cannot eat certain foods. Teach them how to check food labels for themselves.

Adults and children need to drink plenty of water every day. Some studies report that children who are actively encouraged to drink water throughout the day show a rise in their learning retention rates. Try to provide water in the classroom.

Instructions
1   Ask the children what kinds of food people eat for breakfast and write these down.

2   Draw some plates and discuss with the children what some balanced meals for breakfast might be. Then write the foods (or draw them) on the plates.

3   Do the same for different balanced meals for lunch and tea.

4   Reinforce with the children that food gives us energy and our bodies need energy throughout the day. Explain that it is what we eat in our diet overall that is important, not just what we eat for one meal.

5   Invite the children to complete Activity Sheet 17. Explain to them that they are going to 'fill' the lunch box with healthy foods by writing or drawing them on the picture.

Resources
Photocopies of Activity Sheet 17

Extension activities
Devise some healthy sandwich fillings and have a competition for the tastiest sounding idea.
Ask the children to keep a food diary (for a day), writing down all the things they eat and drink throughout the day. Ask them to transfer this information to a set of traffic lights (as explained in Unit 16 'My body needs energy') and check with them what kinds of food and drink they need to have more of.

Yum-Yum by Mick Manning and Brita Granstrom, Wonderwise Books, Franklin Watts.
ISBN 0-7496-3130-9

Choosing lunch

Draw or write the food you would include to make a healthy packed lunch in the lunch box.

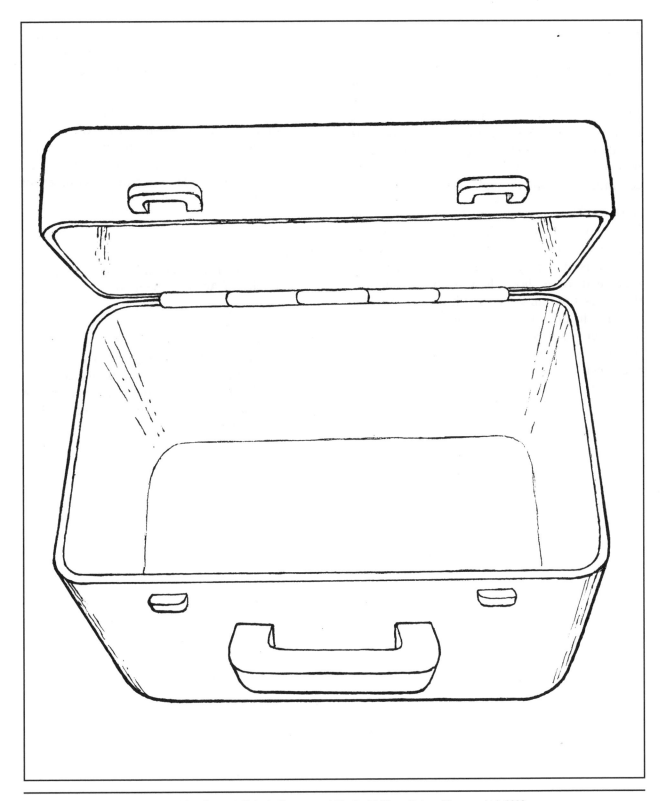

Eating and exercise

18 Keeping fit and well

Aims
- To develop an understanding of the importance of exercise in keeping our bodies fit and well.
- To enable children to recognise different forms of exercise.

Teaching points
Children do not always recognise some kinds of 'play' activities as also being forms of exercise, for example playing football, dancing or skipping. They sometimes see 'exercise' as work which has to be done rather than something enjoyable. It is important to explore this perception as we want children to see exercise as part and parcel of their everyday lives and to continue exercising throughout their lives.

In the early years, children will benefit by being shown how to play active games at playtimes and lunchtimes. Do not assume children understand how to use the playground markings to play – they need to be shown how. Although initially this takes time and energy, ultimately children are able to play more independently and there are fewer playground disputes. Learning to play together is an important aspect of citizenship and social development.

Instructions
1. Distribute a sheet of paper to each child and ask them to draw and/or write down as many different kinds of exercise as they can think of.

2. Review the children's ideas and draw up a list of the different kinds of exercise they have thought of. Suggest any ideas that they have not thought of.

3. Discuss 'play' activities and how some of them are forms of exercise and some are not, for example playing with a PlayStation® is not a form of exercise; playing football is.

4. Ask the children why they think we need to exercise. (To strengthen our bodies and help keep ourselves fit. To keep our hearts strong so that they can pump oxygen around our bodies.)

5. Invite the children to complete Activity Sheet 18 by writing or drawing the kinds of exercise they enjoy and what they do each day of the week.

6. Review by asking the children to share some of their favourite forms of exercise. Encourage the children to try to get some form of exercise every day by playing an active game at playtimes and lunchtimes for example.

Resources
1 sheet of paper for each child
Photocopies of Activity Sheet 18

Extension activities
Involve the lunchtime supervisory staff in understanding the value of exercise for children. Work with them to develop some playground activities that they can teach the children. This may also help with discipline issues.

Ask the children to talk with their parents/carers/grandparents about games they used to play as children and make a class book of traditional playground activities.

 Am I Fit and Healthy? Learning about Diet and Exercise by Claire Llewellyn, Wayland Publishers Ltd.
ISBN 0-7502-2330-8

Keeping fit and well

Draw and write your favourite kinds of exercise.

Think about the kinds of exercise you do during most weeks. Draw or write the exercise you do next to the day of the week on which you do it.

MONDAY

FRIDAY

TUESDAY

SATURDAY

WEDNESDAY

SUNDAY

THURSDAY

Eating and exercise

19 Together, on my own, indoors or outdoors

Aims
- To develop an understanding of forms of exercise that can be done independently and forms of exercise that are done with other people.
- To consider exercise that can take place indoors and exercise that can take place outdoors.
- To develop an understanding of why exercise is important, especially helping to keep our hearts healthy.
- To raise awareness of the importance of including water in our daily diet.

Teaching points
Much of this topic can be reinforced in PE lessons. Check that all staff delivering PE lessons are up-to-date with their knowledge of 'safe' exercise for children. Messages can be reinforced by taking the time to explain to the children what is happening to their bodies while they are exercising, why there is a need to do warm-up and warm-down activities, how the exercise is of benefit to their muscles, bones and organs. Most importantly, children need to enjoy it!

Instructions
1   Generate two lists with the children: one list showing exercise that can be done independently and one list showing exercise that has to be done with other people.
   (The children can work in groups to generate the lists if you prefer.)

2   Discuss the different forms of exercise and ask the children why we exercise. (To enjoy it, because it is part of playing with other people, to help to keep us healthy …)

3   Ask the children what happens when we exercise (we get out of breath, we get hot and sweaty, our hearts beat faster, we get thirsty …). Explain to the children that exercising makes our hearts work hard so they get exercised as well and that our hearts need to have some exercise every day to keep strong.

4   Ask the children if they know why we get thirsty when we exercise and explain that we all need to drink plenty of water every day. (See also Extension activities below.)

5   Go back to the two lists of exercise and ask the children which exercises are usually done indoors and which ones are done outdoors. Discuss the benefits of taking fresh air into our lungs when we exercise outdoors.

6   Invite the children to complete Activity Sheet 19, as a review of the discussion.

Resources
Photocopies of Activity Sheet 19

Extension activities
Recent studies show that actively encouraging children and adults to drink plenty of water throughout the day increases their ability to concentrate and increases their learning rate. Try to provide the children with access to water in the classroom and ask your lunchtime staff to provide plenty of water and to actively encourage the children to drink it.

Discuss the Olympic Games and Paralympic Games – the children can devise a children's Olympic Games saying what they would include and why.

Name .... Date ....

Together, on my own, indoors or outdoors

Write or draw 3 kinds of exercise that you can do on your own.

Write or draw 3 kinds of exercise that you can do with other people.

Write or draw 3 kinds of exercise you might do indoors.

Write or draw 3 kinds of exercise you might do outdoors.

Blueprints PSHE and Citizenship Key Stage 1 © Judy Hunter and Sheila Phillips, Nelson Thornes Ltd, 2002

Looking good and keeping well

20 Smile

Aims
- To develop an understanding of what kinds of food and drink can damage teeth if eaten in excess.
- To help children to understand how valuable their teeth are and to encourage them to take care of their teeth.

Teaching points
Children need to be encouraged to eat fewer sugary foods without being given the message that they can never eat them. Encourage the children to see these foods as something that they eat occasionally rather than regularly.

Ensure you take the circumstances of your school into account – whether there is a tuck shop, whether school meals are provided and if so what foods are provided in the school meals, and so on.

Instructions
1 Ask the children if they have always had teeth. Why don't young babies have teeth? (They do not need them for chewing as they do not eat solid foods.)

2 Explain that the first teeth we get are called 'milk teeth' and these usually start to fall out when we are about six or seven years old to make room for the permanent second teeth, which are stronger. Who has lost any of their milk teeth?

3 Discuss what things would be more difficult to do if we didn't have any teeth. (Chewing, biting, smiling, whistling, laughing, speaking, singing ...) Explain that we need to take care of our teeth because they are special to us and because we do not grow any more after our permanent teeth have grown.

4 One way we can look after our teeth is to eat and drink plenty of foods/drinks that are good for our teeth and less of foods/drinks that are not so good for our teeth. Generate two lists with the children – a list of foods and drinks that are good for our teeth and a list of foods and drinks that are not so good for our teeth.

5 In what other ways can we look after our teeth? (Brushing our teeth well every morning and every night or even after every meal, not eating between meals, going to the dentist so that he/she can check our teeth regularly, not biting hard or sharp objects.) Agree with the children some simple 'rules for keeping our teeth healthy' and write these up for the children to copy on Activity Sheet 20.

6 Invite the children to complete Activity Sheet 20 by writing or drawing five things that are kind to teeth, 'Tooth friends', and five things that are not so kind to teeth, 'Tooth enemies'. They can then copy down the 'rules for keeping our teeth healthy'.

Resources
Pictures of different kinds of food and drink to help generate discussion
Photocopies of Activity Sheet 20

Extension activities
Invite someone from your local dental health service to come into school. They will often bring toothbrushes and show the children how to brush their teeth properly as well as discussing with them how to take care of their teeth.

 The Shark Who Bit Things He Shouldn't by Denis Bond, Little Hippo Scholastic Books. ISBN 0-590-54322-9

Name.. Date ....

Smile

Draw or write 5 things that are kind to your teeth.

Draw or write 5 things that are not so kind to your teeth.

Tooth friends

Tooth enemies

Copy the **"Rules for keeping our teeth healthy"**.

....

....

....

....

....

....

Blueprints PSHE and Citizenship Key Stage I © Judy Hunter and Sheila Phillips, Nelson Thornes Ltd, 2002

Looking good and keeping well

21 Looking after my teeth

Aims

- To reinforce information on caring for our teeth.
- To extend children's knowledge of dental health issues.

Teaching points

Working in partnership with parents is crucial to good dental health education. Don't assume that parents automatically know how to help children care for their teeth – they may not themselves have had sufficient dental health education. Your local dental health service will sometimes deliver sessions for parents or joint parent/child sessions. Alternatively, you can involve parents by making them aware of the school policy on tuck shops and food/drink brought into school by children. Explain the reasons and ask for their co-operation, for example if they usually bring a snack when they collect their children ask them to support the work you are doing by bringing a healthier snack/drink.

Don't give out sweets as a reward for good work – try stickers or merit points instead. If you usually give children sweet prizes in assemblies or treats on their birthdays, try fruit instead. You will be surprised how quickly the children adapt to this.

Instructions

1   Explain to the children that they are going to have a quiz on how to look after their teeth. Divide the children into teams so that they can discuss their answers.

2   Distribute copies of Activity Sheet 21 which contains the quiz questions, reading out one at a time and allowing time for groups to discuss and decide on their answers.

3   Go through the answers with the class, providing any extra information you feel appropriate. You can keep a tally of each team's score if you choose and give some 'kind to teeth' prizes at the end.

Resources

Photocopies of Activity Sheet 21

Extension activities

Collect a range of drinks and foods to show the children (fizzy drinks, fresh fruit drinks, different kinds of sweets, biscuits, cakes, crisps, nuts ...) and compare the amount of sugar contained in each by helping the children to read the food labels. You can compile this information in some simple charts showing how much sugar is in different foods and drinks to display in the class. Assemble a range of foods and drinks on two display tables – one table with food/drinks that are good for your teeth and one table with food/drinks that are not so good for your teeth.

 I Know Why I Brush My Teeth (Sam's Science Series) by Kate Rowan, Walker Books Ltd, ISBN 0-7445-7232-0

Quiz answers:
1 Twice a day
2 Milk and water
3 Carrots, breadsticks, low fat crisps
4 Every 3 months
5 c
6 8
7 Straight after a meal (your teeth will probably be covered with sugary food then anyway)
8 Every 6 or 12 months.

21

Activity Sheet

Looking after my teeth

QUIZ

1 **How often should you brush your teeth? (Put a circle around the correct answer.)**

Once a week	Twice a year	Twice a day
Never	7 times a day	When I remember

2 **Which 2 of these drinks are the healthiest drinks to choose? (Put a circle around the 2 correct answers.)**

Fizzy fruit juice   Milk   Diet cola   Water

3 **Choose 3 healthy snacks to eat from the ones below. (Put a circle around the 3 correct answers.)**

Sweets	Carrots	Chocolate biscuit
Breadsticks	Low fat crisps	Iced cake

4 **How often should you replace your toothbrush?**

Twice a year	When the bristles fall out	Once a year
Every 3 months	When I get my permanent adult teeth	

5 **Eating sweets at playtime can ... (Circle a, b or c to finish the sentence.)**

a Help your teeth to rot.   **b** Make you too full to eat your lunch.

c Help your teeth to rot and make you too full to eat your lunch.

6 **How many teaspoons of sugar are in a can of fizzy cola? (not diet cola)**

None   2   4   8

7 **When is the best time to eat sugary food?**

At meal times   Between meals   Straight after a meal

8 **How often should you visit your dentist so that he/she can check your teeth are keeping healthy?**

Once all your permanent teeth have grown	Every week
Only when you have toothache Every month	Every 6 or 12 months

Looking good and keeping well

22 Keeping clean

Aims

- To develop an understanding of how and why we need to keep ourselves clean.
- To consider how people may be influenced by the way we present ourselves.

Teaching points

We need to try to convey some basic hygiene messages so that children begin to see this as part and parcel of their daily lives. In addition, they can begin to understand that not keeping themselves clean can have consequences, including social consequences, and can impact on their friends and peers. Helping children to understand something of what influences their relationships with others is also part of basic hygiene education.

Wherever possible ensure the whole class washes their hands before lunch, insist that children use handkerchiefs and remind them when they have coughs and sneezes that they need to be as careful as possible not to spread germs.

Instructions

1 Draw an outline of a gingerbread person and tell the children that this is someone who keeps very clean and tidy.

2 Ask the children what this person does to keep himself/herself clean and tidy, and write their answers around the outline.

3 Ask the children: What do other people say about this person?

4 Draw an outline of another gingerbread person and tell the children this is someone who does not take care of himself/herself and is not very clean or tidy.

5 Ask the children what this person looks like, and write their answers around the outline.

6 Ask the children what other people say about this person.

7 Ask and discuss the following questions:

- Do you think it is fair that people say these things about the person who does not take care of himself/herself?
- Do you think it will affect who they are friends with?
- What could be the reasons why this person does not take care of himself/herself?
- We are going to be this person's friend and try to help him/her – what can this person do to take better care of himself/herself?

(The main points to draw out are: washing hands after going to the toilet, before touching or eating food and after touching animals; brushing our teeth; washing by taking baths or showers; using a handkerchief; changing our clothes regularly (especially underwear); washing and brushing our hair and tying back long hair, cleaning under nails and cutting nails regularly.)

8 Invite the children to complete Activity Sheet 22 'A day in the life of Chris Clean'.

Resources

Photocopies of Activity Sheet 22

Extension activities

Do some simple experiments where children wash their hands in cold water only, hot water only, cold water with soap and hot water with soap. What gets the best results (you can use paint on their hands)?

Discuss the different ways that germs can be spread.

The children can design some notices/posters to display in the toilets to remind other children to wash their hands.

 Wash, scrub, brush: a book about keeping clean, by Mick Manning and Brita Granstrom, Wonderwise Books, Franklin Watts.
ISBN 0-7496-3684-X

Name .... Date ....

Keeping clean

Chris Clean is someone who always keeps clean and tidy. Draw a picture
of Chris Clean here.

Finish the story of Chris Clean. Imagine what Chris Clean does to keep
clean and tidy, from the time he gets up in the morning till he goes to bed
at night.

A Day in the Life of Chris Clean

Chris Clean wakes up bright and early one morning, gives a
big stretch, jumps out of bed and …

Feelings and feeling good

23 Finding the words

Aims
- To develop children's vocabulary to include a language of emotions.
- To develop an understanding that everyone has feelings and all feelings are acceptable.
- To develop an understanding that all people feel different things at different times.

Teaching points
Developing emotional intelligence in our children is fundamental to them making good health choices throughout their lives. It is the basis of being able to form and build relationships and communicate effectively within those relationships. The starting point is to help children to develop a language of feelings – not being able to name a feeling can be frustrating and often leaves children with no alternative but to display their feelings through actions rather than words.

Avoid the language of 'positive feelings', 'negative feelings', 'good' and 'bad' feelings. All feelings need to be accepted because they are just an instinctive response to a situation. However, actions as a result of feelings need to be limited and it is therefore to the actions that we can attribute 'right' or 'wrong', 'good' or 'bad'. If we tell a child that a feeling is bad, naughty, wrong, it is unlikely to stop them feeling it instinctively again, but there is a danger that they will then not articulate the feeling and/or feel guilty for feeling it. We do, however, quite clearly need to help children to understand that their feelings influence their actions and behaviour and that certain behaviours are not acceptable despite what they are feeling.

Instructions
1 Generate with the children as many feeling words as possible. Try to extend their vocabulary by asking for alternative words to describe, for example feeling angry, happy, sad, worried, and so on. Write these in a circle.

2 Discuss the words to help the whole class to understand what the words mean. Ask the children how they think feeling a little bit worried might be different to feeling very frightened, feeling really angry might be different to feeling a little bit annoyed, feeling very happy might be different to feeling just OK.

3 Ask the children to complete Activity Sheet 23 by writing words that describe angry feelings, unhappy feelings and happy feelings on the petals of the appropriate flowers, and then write other feelings words on the last flower. They can also draw more flowers if they need to. They can use words they think of or those generated earlier.

Resources
Photocopies of Activity Sheet 23

Extension activities
Cut out some large petals from card and display feeling flowers on the wall as a reminder of the vocabulary.

Encourage the children to identify feelings after activities and at different times in the day/week by asking them to say how they feel about different experiences, for example:

'The best feeling I have had this week was … when …'

'Sometimes in this class I feel sad when …'

'During playtime today I felt …'

 How Do You Feel? by Gillian Liu, Evans Brothers Ltd. ISBN 0-237-51432-X

Name .... Date ....

Finding the words

Write as many words as you can think of to describe **angry** feelings on the petals of this flower.

angry

Write as many words as you can think of to describe **unhappy** feelings on the petals of this flower.

unhappy

Write as many words as you can think of to describe **happy** feelings on the petals of this flower.

happy

Write any other words you can think of about feelings on the petals of this flower.

Feelings and feeling good

24 Please don't shout!

Aims
- To enable children to understand that they have choices over their behaviour and actions.
- To consider appropriate and inappropriate behaviour in response to different feelings and in different situations.

Teaching points
This activity follows on well from 'Finding the words' on pages 46–47 and links with aspects of citizenship. Even very young children can be helped to understand how their feelings influence their behaviour and that they have choices about how to behave. They need to understand the consequences if they choose to behave inappropriately. (These consequences need to be applied consistently within the school environment.)

The 'traffic light' system explained below, also forms part of the activity in 'Should I put it in my mouth?' in the section 'Medicines and Drugs' on page 18.

Instructions
1 Draw a set of traffic lights and ask the children what red, amber and green on traffic lights mean. Explain that they can make decisions by thinking of traffic lights, always stopping to think what they should do before responding to a situation.

   On our traffic lights, red means **stop**, amber means **think** what choices you have, green means **decide** on your best choice.

2 Ask the children to think of a situation in school that might cause them to feel angry. (Alternatively, you can ask them to imagine a scenario such as someone walking up to them at playtime and kicking them for no reason at all.)

3 Apply the situation to the traffic lights – write 'I feel angry' next to red and ask the children what choices they have about how

they respond to the situation. Write the choices next to amber.

4 Discuss the options with the children and encourage them to think about what the consequences of their choices might be. Now ask them what they think the best choice would be and write this next to the green light.

5 This activity can be extended to cover as many feelings and situations as you choose. Exploring the feeling that something is unfair is useful to help children to begin to understand that they can do something positive with such a feeling, and is an excellent citizenship activity.

6 Ask the children to complete Activity Sheet 24 by writing something that sometimes causes them to feel angry at home or when they are playing with their friends and then writing the choices they have against the amber traffic light and their best choice against the green light.

Resources
Photocopies of Activity Sheet 24

Extension activities
Apply the traffic light system to the classroom, for example when the class gets too noisy say 'We are on red now'. This indicates that they should stop. Then ask the children what is happening and what they can do about it (amber). When ready, move on to green.

Follow through the theme of justice by picking up on key news items and ask the children what they think about the situations. They may decide they would like to form links with a particular charity and do something positive.

 This Is Our House by Michael Rosen, Walker Books Ltd. ISBN 0-7445-3750-9

Temper Temper! by Norman Silver, MacDonald Young Books. ISBN 0-7500-2703-7

Name .... Date ....

Please don't shout!

Think of something that sometimes makes you feel angry when you are at home or when you are playing with your friends. Write it down here.

....

....

What can you do? Write all your choices next to the amber light.

Then write what you think is your best choice next to the green light.

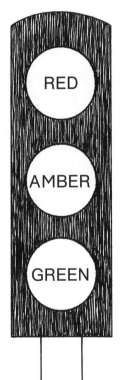 **I feel angry!**

I think the choice I have made is the best choice because ...

....

....

Feelings and feeling good

25 A rainbow of feelings

Aims
- To extend children's vocabulary of emotions.
- To encourage the children to be aware of their feelings and to express them.

Teaching points
If you have already covered the activity 'Finding the words' on pages 46–47, the children will have begun to build their vocabulary of feelings and will now have some words to choose from for this activity. Developing emotional intelligence does not, however, start and stop with activities specifically focused on this aspect of PSHE. We need to seek opportunities to reinforce this work by encouraging children to say how they feel about situations and experiences in school. For example, ask the children at the end of a school day how they feel looking back on the day, ask them how they feel about a particular piece of work they have done, how they feel about something topical in the news or a school event. Circle time is an ideal opportunity for this. Try not to avoid the sometimes sensitive feelings associated with grief and loss, children will experience these feelings at some time in their lives and it is better to prepare them for that time.

N.B. Be aware that you need to be sensitive about the word 'black' in Instruction 3 below and of the implications this may have if there are children from different races in your class.

Instructions
1 Select a range of musical instruments and encourage the children to listen carefully and use words to describe the different sounds (tinkly, jangly, smooth, deep ...).

2 Now ask them to think about how they feel when they hear each one. Ask and discuss with the children: Do some sounds help us to feel in different ways? Are there any sounds which can be peaceful, frightening, sad, happy ...?

3 Ask the children if they associate any words to describe feelings with different colours. If you think of a bright, yellow colour, what feeling word might you associate with it? Discuss words associated with other colours.

4 Invite the children to complete Activity Sheet 25 by colouring in the rainbow and writing in some feeling words for each of the different colours.

Resources
Musical instruments
Coloured pencils
Photocopies of Activity Sheet 25

Extension activities
Make a rainbow for the classroom wall, writing across it words to describe feelings. Ask the children to bring in some ribbons of as many different colours and textures as possible. These can be used to make a display and extend children's vocabulary by asking them for words to describe the ribbons: smooth, velvety, sparkly, shiny, slinky. They can also add any feeling words they choose.

Poems About Feeling selected by Amanda Earl and Danielle Sensier, Wayland Publishers Ltd.
ISBN 0-7502-0972-0

A rainbow of feelings

Colour in the rainbow below and then write words to describe any feelings you might have when you think of each colour.

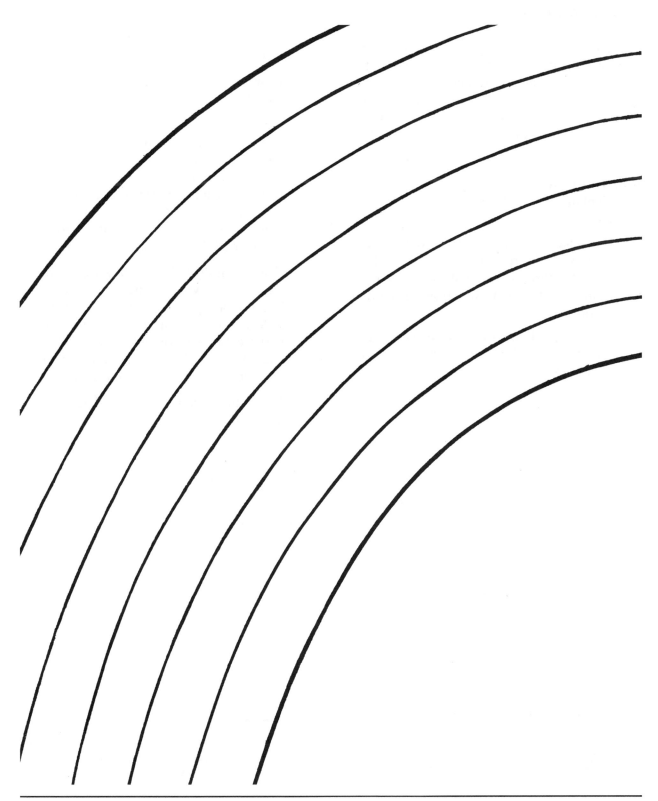

Feelings and feeling good

26 Other people have feelings too

Aims

- To help children to understand that the words they use and the actions they take may affect the feelings of other people.
- To begin to develop the skill of empathy.

Teaching points

Children can often be so engaged in their own world and their own feelings that they are simply unaware of the need to consider what the consequences of their words and actions on other people might be. They therefore need to learn this skill – it is not necessarily something that they will either be born with or develop instinctively.

Instructions

1 Explain the following scenario to the children:

'Leon has just heard that he is going away to camp with the rest of his class. He will be away for three nights and has never been away from home or away from his mother before.'

Ask the children to imagine what Leon might be feeling and write down the children's words.

anxious
grown-up
curious
frightened
worried
happy
excited

2 Discuss with the children that one person might feel very frightened about something while another feels very excited about it – a bit like a ride on a rollercoaster.

3 Explain to the children that Leon's best friend, Joseph, is also going on the trip and says to Leon that they will have a great time because he has heard that everyone stays up really late and tells scary stories. Discuss with the children how Joseph might be feeling about going on the trip.

4 Ask and discuss how Leon might be feeling about what Joseph said.

5 'The class is soon due to go to camp and Leon brings a note from his mother into school. The note says that Leon will now not be going on the school trip. Leon looks very unhappy when he hands over the note to the teacher.'

Ask the children for possible reasons why Leon might not be going.

6 Discuss whether what Joseph said could have affected Leon being able to go to camp.

How would different people in the class have felt if Joseph had said that to them?

7 Finally, explain to the children that Leon had always been really looking forward to going to camp and became even more excited by what Joseph said to him. The reason he cannot go is because the week of the school camp clashes with a family holiday on which he also wants to go. Who is surprised that this was the reason?

8 Discuss with the children how we can never know exactly what another person is feeling because all people and all feelings are different, but we can try to understand as best we can how other people are feeling and think carefully about how our words and actions might affect their feelings.

9 Invite the children to complete Activity Sheet 26.

Resources

Photocopies of Activity Sheet 26

Extension activities

You can add any new feeling words that have arisen through this activity for display in the classroom.

Ask the children to think of some situations where different people might feel different things.

Worried Arthur by Joan Stimson, Ladybird Books Ltd. ISBN 0-7214-3538-8

Something Else by Kathryn Cave, Penguin Books. ISBN 0-670-84892-1

Other people have feelings too

Look at the 4 pictures of Leon and Joseph playing football together. What do you think Leon and Joseph might be feeling in each picture?

Write the words for those feelings in the clouds at the bottom of the page.

Friendships, families and being me

27 Being a friend

Aims

- To develop an understanding of the importance of friendships and the responsibilities we have within friendships.
- To develop an understanding of what can build friendships and what can break friendships.

Teaching points

Children need to be encouraged to take responsibility for their actions within friendships and to develop the skills to work and play in harmony with others. Children respond instinctively to their emotions and, with support, can learn to consider how their responses and actions will influence their relationships before taking action.

Instructions

1   Discuss with the children what an 'ideal friend' might be. Write key words around an outline of a person and label the person 'my ideal friend'.

2   Ask the children in what ways they feel they are a good friend. What do they do and say that makes them a good friend? What are the kinds of thing they sometimes do or say that makes them not always such a good friend?

3   What are the kinds of thing that sometimes break friendships? Ask the children to act out some of these things for the rest of the class and then discuss what happened or what was said, and how things could be made better.

4   Invite the children to complete Activity Sheet 27 by picking from the shelf the five qualities they feel are the most important for a friend to have and writing them on the items in the shopping basket. They can then complete the two sentences on the bottom of the page – 'I am a good friend when ...' and 'I am not such a good friend when ...'.

Resources

Photocopies of Activity Sheet 27

Extension activities

The children can think of ways of building good friendships in the class which can then be made into a class friendship charter. For example, 'Let other people join in your games at playtimes', 'Be kind to each other.'

Little Beaver and The Echo by Amy MacDonald, Walker Books Ltd.
ISBN 0-7445-2315-X

What are friends for? by Sally Grindley and Penny Dann, Kingfisher Publications.
ISBN 0-7534-0179-1

Being a friend

From the supermarket shelf below, choose the 5 things that you think are the most important things for a friend to have. Write them on the items in the shopping basket.

A friend is ...

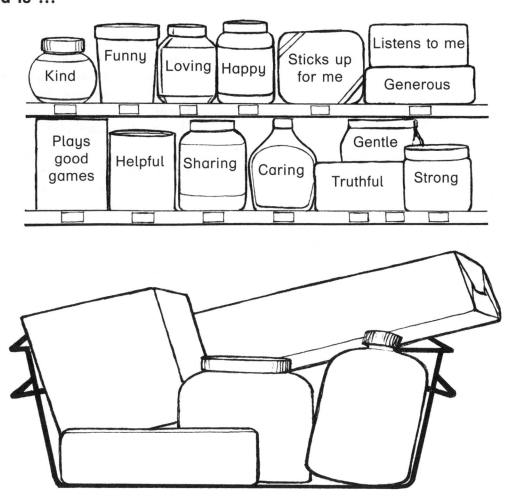

Complete these two sentences.

I am a good friend when ....

....

I am not such a good friend when ....

....

Friendships, families and being me

28 Helpful words and actions

Aims

- To help children to understand that they need people to help them and that they also need to help other people.
- To help children to understand that they are part of their relationships with their families and friends and will have an influence on how those relationships function.

Teaching points

Be sensitive to the many different kinds of families that children will be part of and make the language as inclusive as possible, i.e. do not automatically say 'mother and father', 'grandparents', etc. Children may see their families in terms of a small number of people in their immediate circle or a much wider extended family group. If children have recently suffered the loss of a family member through death, divorce, separation or perhaps because a family member is working away from home, they may have very heightened emotions. This does not mean, however, that the topic should be avoided – it will need sensitive handling but children sometimes need the opportunity to talk about such things.

Instructions

1   Ask the children to think about which people are part of their families and to draw those people on a piece of paper, putting themselves in the middle.

2   Ask some of the children to share who is part of their family with the rest of the class and then ask everyone to write on their drawings all the things they can think of that their family members do to help them. (They can do this individually or in small groups.)

3   Invite the children to share their responses and draw up a list of all the things that their family members do to help them.

4   Now ask the children to write all the things that they do to help members of their families around the drawings of themselves, working either individually or in small groups.

5   Invite the children to share their responses and draw up a list of all the things that they do to help their families.

6   How do their families feel when the children help them in some way?

   - Can anybody think of more ways in which they could help their families?
   - What are the kinds of things they do that are sometimes not helpful to their families?
   - How do their families feel then?

7   Invite the children to complete Activity Sheet 28 and then ask each child in turn to share one way in which they are going to try to help their families more over the next week.

Resources

1 sheet of A4 paper for every child
Photocopies of Activity Sheet 28

Extension activities

Review with the children whether they did what they said they would do to try to help their families more. What happened? How did they feel?

Consider ways in which everyone could help each other in the class and make these into a class promise list.

Five Minutes Peace by Jill Murphy, Walker Books Ltd. ISBN 0-7445-6002-1

Helpful words and actions

Finish the following sentences.

Sometimes I am not helpful to my family when

....

....

....

I think they feel ....

I am helpful to my family when

....

....

....

I think they feel ....

I am going to try to be more helpful to my family this week by

....

....

....

I think they will feel ....

I will feel ....

Blueprints PSHE and Citizenship Key Stage I © Judy Hunter and Sheila Phillips, Nelson Thornes Ltd, 2002

Friendships, families and being me

29 This is me!

Aims
● To enable children to reflect on their uniqueness and value.

Teaching points
In order for children (and adults) to be able to make healthy choices and informed decisions in their lives they need to value themselves. This activity also links with aspects of citizenship – celebrating similarities and differences, taking care of me/taking care of others.

Instructions
1   Display 5 objects at the front of the class (for example a ball, a book, a picture, a scarf, a shoe …) and ask the children how each one is special in its own way, what each one can be used for, whether there are any similarities between the objects (for example the book and the picture may both be nice to look at, the scarf and the shoe can both keep parts of our bodies warm …).

2   Draw up two lists with the children – one list showing how people are/can be similar and the other showing how people are/can be different (colour of hair, eyes, height, gender, hobbies/interests …).

3   Ask the children whether anyone in the world is exactly the same as another person and discuss how everyone in the class is different in some way.

4   Invite the children to tell the rest of the class something they have that is very special to them (for example a pet, a toy …) and explain how they take care of the special thing(s) in their lives.

5   Now ask the children to share anything they can think of that helps to make them special.

6   As we are so very special, how can we take care of ourselves? Draw up a list with the children.

7   Invite the children to complete Activity Sheet 29 by building up a profile of themselves and focusing on what makes them special and unique.

Resources
5 objects (see Instruction 1 above)
Photocopies of Activity Sheet 29

Extension activities
Explore how everyone's thumbprint is unique.

Ask the children to do a self-portrait of themselves and then, working in groups of 4 or 5, ask each member of the group to write something positive under each other's portrait that helps to make that person special and unique.

 All Kinds of People by Emma Damon, Tango Books.
ISBN 1-857-07067-4

Name .... Date ....

This is me!

Fill in your answers in the spaces below.

My name is .... My age is ....

The colour of my eyes is .... The colour of my hair is ....

My skin colour is .... My favourite food is ....

My hobbies are ....

My favourite book is ....

Something that is very special to me is ....

Something that makes me very special is ....

....

Because I am very special, I take care of myself by ....

....

....

....

Friendships, families and being me

30 Sharing and caring

Aims
- To help children to understand that most people worry about something at some time in their lives and that if they have worries they are not alone.
- To help children to understand that sharing a worry with someone often helps us to cope better with the worry and the feelings related to it.
- To enable children to begin to develop the skill of empathy with other people's concerns and feelings.

Teaching points
It is important not to give the message that all worries can be resolved and that sharing them will make them go away – this is not always the case, but sharing can often help people to cope better with the worry. Some children will not share their worries at home because they do not want to hurt or cause concern to their families and it can therefore often be safer to share them in school through an activity such as this one. It is worth collecting a few books for individual use on particular issues that can arise, such as moving schools, moving home, the birth of a sibling, and so on.

Instructions
1   Discuss with the children what different kinds of thing adults and children might worry about.

2   If someone is worried about something, what sort of things could that person or other people do to try to ease the worry?

3   Read the following scenarios to the children and ask them to share what could be done to try to ease these worries. After each one, discuss what the best option might be and why they think that.

(a)   'Jon does not enjoy coming to school. He worries all the time about not being very good at his work, not being as good as other people at sport and not having many friends to play with at playtime.'

(b)   'Lucy hears her family arguing a lot at home and lies in bed worrying about it. She wants to stop them but doesn't know what to do and is frightened that she could make it worse.'

(c)   'Rudi has to take medicine every day, both in school and at home. He has to use an inhaler in school and also has two spoonfuls of medicine every lunchtime. He worries about the other children calling him names and talking about him.'

4   Invite the children to complete Activity Sheet 30.

N.B. Do check the children's activity sheets for any concerns/disclosures that may be expressed through this activity and follow them up sensitively and within your school child protection guidelines.

Resources
Photocopies of Activity Sheet 30

Extension activities
Devise additional scenarios for the children to respond to or ask the children to make up examples of their own.

The above (or additional) scenarios can be turned into role-play activities if you prefer the children to act out their responses.

Ask the children to devise '5 handy hints' to help with worries.

The Huge Bag Of Worries by Virginia Ironside, MacDonald Young Books.
ISBN 0-7500-2124-1

There Is No Such Thing as a Dragon by Jack Kent, Happy Cat Books.
ISBN 1-899248-95-1

Sharing and caring

Write what worries these children might have in their thought bubbles above their heads. They are about the same age as you.

I think what would help most with these children's worries ....

....

....

....

If I ever have a worry, I ....

....

....

....

The environment

31 Looking around us

Aims
- To develop an understanding of what the word 'environment' means.
- To heighten children's perceptions of the world around them in terms of environmental issues.

Teaching points
To us, perhaps, there is clearly a link between the environment and our health and quality of life. To children this may be less obvious and they need to be encouraged to see that being in control of their health, in terms of choices and decisions, means also considering the environmental factors that can influence their health.

Environmental education incorporates teaching the skills of risk assessment and links with aspects of citizenship. The 'Keeping safer' section on pages 22–31 also overlaps with some of these issues.

Instructions
1   Ask the children what the word 'environment' means to them and write down their ideas. Ask them to think about the environment they are in now and other environments that they go into.

2   Discuss with the children what makes an environment a nice place to be.

   What makes it a not so nice place to be?

3   Focus on the school environment by writing down the word 'school' and asking the children to name all the people who have a part to play in helping to make the school environment a nice place to be (see diagram at the top of the next column).

4   Discuss with the children the part that each person plays and how they can help to make school a nice place to be or a not so nice place to be.

5   Ask the children to look carefully around the classroom – what are the things that help

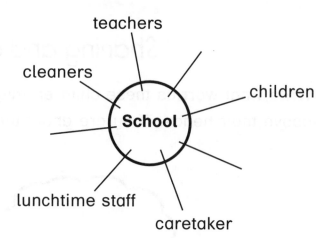

to make this environment a pleasant one? What can everyone do to help to make this a better environment? Collect the ideas and, if you wish, make them into a list to display on the wall as a reminder to the children.

6   Invite the children to complete Activity Sheet 31, drawing and writing what kind of things make their classroom a nice environment to be in, and what could make their classroom a better environment to be in.

Resources
Photocopies of Activity Sheet 31

Extension activities
Vote on the suggestions to improve the classroom environment to see which are the most popular. Which ones can be carried out with little or no financial implications? Explore with the children which ones have financial implications, and which are realistic/unrealistic and why. Write a class letter to the headteacher or governors saying how everyone in the class is going to help to keep the classroom environment a pleasant place to be, and ask for support in improving it if there is one thing that has a small cost implication.

A New Home for Tiger by Joan Stimson, Scholastic Children's Books. ISBN 0-590-54194-3

Looking around us

What makes your classroom a nice environment to be in? Complete the sentence and the drawing below.

My classroom is a nice environment because ....

....

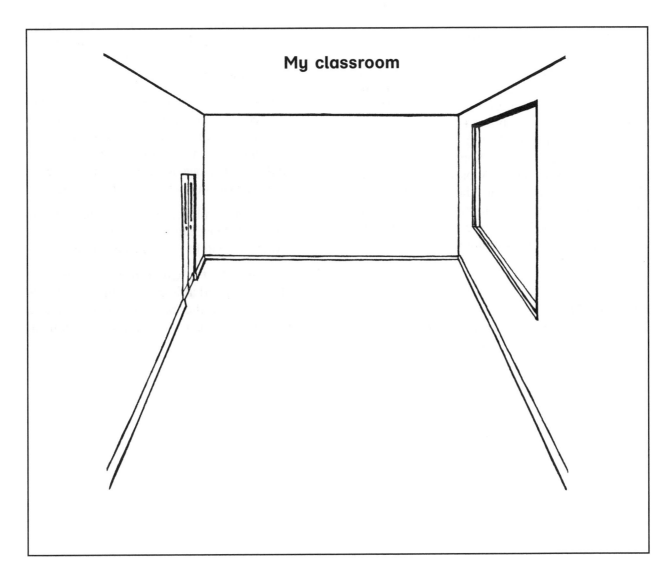

My classroom

What could make it an even nicer environment to be in? Add this to your drawing and complete the sentence.

I think this classroom could be made into a nicer environment if.................

....

....

Blueprints PSHE and Citizenship Key Stage I © Judy Hunter and Sheila Phillips, Nelson Thornes Ltd, 2002

The environment

32 The school community

Aims
- To begin to develop the skills of risk assessment.
- To raise awareness that everyone can contribute to maintaining a safe and pleasant school environment.

Teaching points
The best way to develop awareness of environmental issues and responsible attitudes towards those issues, is to provide opportunities for children to live out our messages by putting them into practice. Consider, therefore, how children are encouraged to save resources in school (water and energy for example). What provision is made to support recycling? Do you have facilities for can collection, for example, or separation of rubbish into appropriate bins for collection? If this becomes part and parcel of children's lives at school, they are likely to spread the messages at home and encourage other members of their families to consider their contribution to the environment.

Instructions
1 Nominate some key places within school for the class to consider how safe and pleasant each environment is, for example the toilets, corridors, playground and dining hall. Divide the children into groups and allocate each group one of those places to consider. (Alternatively, you can work with the whole class to consider each place in turn.)

2 Ask each group to draw up two lists – one showing what helps to make that environment a safe and pleasant place and one showing what helps to make it not such a safe and pleasant place to be. (It is helpful if the children can actually go into the environment to draw up their lists.)

3 Ask all the groups to feed back their views and discuss each place. Identify anything that the children think might not be very safe and use a scale to help the children to assess the level of risk of each item as follows:

   1 Very unsafe
   2 A little unsafe
   3 Fairly safe
   4 Safe
   5 Very safe

4 Agree on one or two priorities that emerge from assessing the level of risk and discuss what could be done to help to make their environment safer.

5 This information can be fed back through the school council and feedback given to the children on what action will be taken. Alternatively, the children can present their findings and suggestions to the headteacher or governors in verbal or written form.

6 Invite the children to complete Activity Sheet 32. They can formulate a list of rules either in small groups or as a whole class.

7 Discuss with the children which rules can also be applied at home and in other places and reinforce the message that they have a part to play in caring for their environment.

Resources
Photocopies of Activity Sheet 32

Extension activities
The children can involve parents/carers by composing a letter asking them to contribute to making the school environment a safe and pleasant place to be.

Name... Date ....

The school community

We all need to help to keep our school a safe and pleasant place to be.

This is what we are all going to try to do to help.

Our rules for keeping school a safe and pleasant place to be

The environment

33 The world is precious

Aims
- To enable children to consider environmental issues in different situations which can have different consequences.
- To develop the skill of risk assessment.

Teaching points
The book recommended for this activity can be used as a means of reviewing issues or stimulating discussion at the beginning of the activity. It contains the message 'The world is precious, every bit – please don't make a mess of it'. The children can make posters using this message for display around the school.

Instructions
1 Ask the children to imagine they are going for a walk through the park on a lovely summer's day. What are all the nice things they might see, hear and smell in the park as they walk through it? What does it feel like to be there? (It is useful to write down the vocabulary as this can be used for English extension work.)

2 Now ask them to imagine that they are going through the same park the next day, but during the night some people have been in the park and done lots of things to try to spoil it. What might we now see, hear and smell as we go through the park? What does it feel like to be there?

3 Discuss with the children what might be the consequences of some of the things that have spoilt the park (in terms of people's enjoyment, people's feelings, their health and safety).

4 Ask the children:
- Why do you think the people chose to spoil it?
- What could happen now to put it right?
- Who will put it right?
- Who will pay to put it right? (This is an opportunity for children to consider the financial implications of acts of vandalism.)

5 Invite the children to complete Activity Sheet 33 by considering what might be the possible consequences of each of the scenarios shown in the pictures.

6 Review the work by inviting the children to share their answers and remind them that they all have a responsibility to keep their environment safe and pleasant.

Resources
Photocopies of Activity Sheet 33

Extension activities
If possible, take the children to a local park or an area of the city and ask them to identify all the possible risks to the environment. Discuss what preventative action could be taken, focusing particularly on whose responsibility it is.

Ask the children to design and make some posters about ways of helping to keep different environments safe.

 Lottie's Letter by Gordon Snell and Peter Bailey, Orion Children's Books.
ISBN 1-85881-187-2

The world is precious

Look at each picture. What is happening? Write down what you think might happen next.

What could happen here?

....

....

What could happen here?

....

....

What could happen here?

....

....

What could happen here?

....

....

What could happen here?

....

....

What could happen here?

....

....

Blueprints PSHE and Citizenship Key Stage I © Judy Hunter and Sheila Phillips, Nelson Thornes Ltd, 2002

The environment

34 The wider picture

Aims
- To begin to develop an awareness of wider global environmental issues.
- To enable children to consider how they can make a positive contribution in relation to those issues.

Teaching points
It can be difficult for children to think beyond their immediate environment, especially for children who have never travelled far from home. So it is a good idea to link this with some geography work to enable children to develop some understanding of where they live in this country and where this country is in relation to other countries. The work could coincide with introducing work on rural and urban environments, or hot and cold environments.

Instructions
1   Discuss with the children what basic things we need in our lives (food, water, clothing and shelter to keep us warm and dry), and explore how these are different to the things we might want in our lives.

2   Explain that we rely on our environment for our needs and, as an example, generate a list with the children of all the things we need. What would happen if we did not have water?

3   Discuss the origins and uses of other materials, for example where does a wool jumper start from, leather shoes, paper, wood to build houses? What are chips made from? Where do the potatoes come from?

4   Explain to the children that when a tree is cut down another one has to be planted so that we will continue to have the resources we need. We have to take care of our environment but not everyone does this. Ask the children to think of as many different ways as they can in which people waste water. (They can do this in small groups, pairs or as a whole class.)

5   Invite the children to work individually or in small groups to design an advertisement on Activity Sheet 34 which will help to sell the idea of saving water.

If you wish, you can bring in examples of advertisements and discuss them with the children first. (The children can design the advertisement using a computer if you prefer.)

6   Review the ideas the children have come up with for their advertisements.

Resources
Examples of advertisements (see Instruction 5 above)
Photocopies of Activity Sheet 34

Extension activities
Explore all the uses of wood with the children and explore what is happening in the rainforests. Collect newspaper headlines and extracts of articles to help expand the children's thinking and understanding of environmental issues.

Explore where different food products come from and their different uses. What are the basic ingredients in some foods? What are some different ways we can cook and use potatoes? Remind the children of the different foods we need in our diets.

 Madeleine the City Pig by Karen Wallace, Macmillan Children's Books.
ISBN 0-333-73945-0

Rachel's Roses by Karen Christensen, Barefoot Books.
ISBN 1-901223-57-4

The wider picture

Design an advertisement to help encourage people to save water. Draw and write it in the box below.

WANTED – *people to help save water*

SAVE WATER

SAVE WATER

SAVE WATER

SAVE WATER

SAVE WATER

SAVE WATER

SAVE WATER

SAVE WATER

Everyone needs to help look after our environment.

Citizenship

35 What are rules for?

Aims

- To raise awareness of the importance of a system/society where people live to a set of rules.
- To encourage the children to consider the rules to which they are expected to adhere, and the possible consequences of not adhering to those rules.

Teaching points

Whilst schools will generally have an established set of rules which can be made explicit to the children, if we wish children to develop independence, responsibility and to behave appropriately within and beyond school, we need to provide opportunities for them to explore and set their own rules. In the very early years many children will respond to the security of established rules, but we must never assume they fully understand their meaning. Every child comes from a different family and therefore, in a sense, a different culture. All families will have slightly different rules and slightly different definitions of acceptable behaviour. Take the time to explore why the classroom and school rules are in place and what they mean in terms of behaviour that will be deemed appropriate and acceptable. As children mature and settle into school life, they will be able to begin to define their own set of rules in addition to complying with your rules and the school rules.

Instructions

1 Discuss the meaning of the word 'rule' with the children. Ask them what rules a newly born baby would be expected to keep. (None) Why is a newly born baby not expected to keep to any rules?

2 What rules would a two-year-old child be expected to keep? Why is this? (Raise the issues of needing to keep a two-year-old child safe and helping him/her to develop appropriate types of behaviour. Ask the children what 'appropriate' types of behaviour might be for a two-year-old child.)

3 Ask the children what rules they are expected to keep in school and outside school and draw up two lists. (They can work in small groups first to generate ideas if you prefer.)

4 Discuss the lists with the children, exploring why each rule is needed and what might be the consequences if the rule was not there or they did not keep it. Highlight the fact that as we grow older we are expected to behave in increasingly responsible ways and to keep to rules without needing to be reminded.

5 Review your classroom rules with the children and ask them if they feel they would like to add any more. Discuss any ideas they come up with and if all the class agrees you can add the new rules.

6 Invite the children to complete Activity Sheet 35, focusing on what rules are needed for happy and safe playtimes.

7 Review with the children what rules they feel are important for playtimes and why.

Resources

Photocopies of Activity Sheet 35

Extension activities

Invite some of your lunchtime supervisory staff into the classroom to talk with the children about what rules they feel are important at lunchtimes and in the playground, and why. Together, you can discuss how the children would like their lunchtimes to operate and what they enjoy and do not enjoy about them.

Carrot Tops and Cottontails by Jan Mark, Diamond Books. ISBN 0-261-67167-7

Tusk Tusk by David McKee, Red Fox. ISBN 0-09-930650-6

What are rules for?

Draw and write what you like to do at playtime.

At playtime I like to

Draw and write what can sometimes spoil playtimes.

Sometimes playtimes are spoilt because

Write which rules you think are good rules to have at playtime.

My **GOLDEN** rules for playtime

Blueprints PSHE and Citizenship Key Stage I © Judy Hunter and Sheila Phillips, Nelson Thornes Ltd, 2002

Citizenship

36 That hurts!

Aims
- To consider the consequences of hurtful and damaging actions.
- To enable children to reflect on their own actions and words.

Teaching points
This activity also focuses on developing the skill of empathy and links with the section 'Feelings and feeling good'. The traffic light system, outlined on page 18 can once again be used to reinforce the message of stopping to consider the possible consequence of our actions before making a decision. Helping children to understand that they are responsible for their own behaviour will help them to deal better with moral dilemmas later in life. If children only ever rely on being told how to behave and their behaviour is always controlled externally, they may have difficulty later in life in behaving independently and responsibly.

Instructions
1   Invite the children to complete Activity Sheet 36 by first of all drawing something that is very special to them and describing how they might feel if someone damaged it deliberately.

2   In the second half of the sheet, ask them to draw someone who is special to them and to describe how they might feel if someone hurt that person or that person's feelings.

3   Discuss with the children what they have drawn and write up all the words they have used to describe their feelings. (Remind the children that this is one reason why we need to have 'rules'.)

4   Ask the children to work in small groups and write down all the things that people in school can sometimes say or do which can hurt other people. (Instruct them not to name anyone or make it too personal.)

5   Review the above with the children and then ask them to write down all the things that people in school can sometimes say or do that can help other people.

6   Review the above with the children. Ask each group to choose two things from their list of 'hurtful' actions and words, and two things from their list of 'helpful' actions and words.

7   Ask the children to now write their agreed hurtful words and actions onto two of the pre-cut spiky shapes (see Resources) and their helpful words and actions onto two of the pre-cut smooth shapes and display them in the classroom.

Resources
Pre-cut spiky shapes and smooth shapes for Instruction 7 above

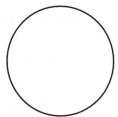

Photocopies of Activity Sheet 36

Extension activities
Go round the class asking each child to add a sentence (or part of a sentence) to a story about someone who is being bullied. Start the story in whatever way you chose. For example: 'Max was standing alone in the playground – he was nearly always alone – around the corner came Laura, Nicky and Rhajit. Max's face turned white with fear and the next minute ...' Explore what happened in the story with the children and discuss what might have helped Max.

The Selfish Crocodile by Faustin Charles, Bloomsbury Publishing Plc.
ISBN 0-7475-4193-0

Two Monsters by David McKee, Red Fox.
ISBN 0-09-945530-7

Name .... Date ....

That hurts!

Draw something that is special to you in the box here.

This is my _____

In the circles below write in some words to describe how you might feel if someone damaged what you have drawn on purpose.

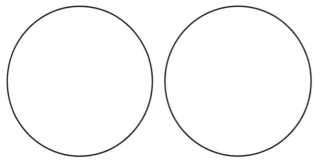

Draw someone who is special to you in the box here.

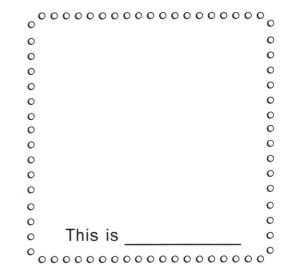

This is _____

In the circles below write in some words to describe how you might feel if someone hurt the person you have drawn or hurt his or her feelings on purpose.

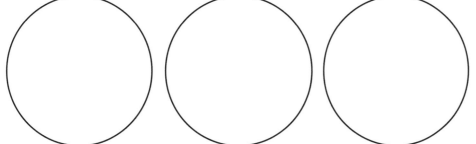

37 Being truthful

Aims

- To explore what being truthful means and what might stop us being truthful.
- To explore the possible consequences of not being truthful.

Teaching points

Children may see that choosing not to tell the truth can protect them from getting into trouble in some instances. They need to be helped to see that not telling the truth can have longer term consequences – it can damage friendships and relationships because people feel they cannot trust. Children also need to be helped to develop the skill of predicting possible outcomes and consequences in terms of keeping themselves and others safe – if, for example, they did not tell the truth about a friend who had taken some medicine he/she should not have taken.

Instructions

1   Discuss with the children what being truthful means. Why do people not always tell the truth? How would you feel if you found out that someone had not been telling you the truth about something? What if this was your best friend?

2   Discuss what people mean when they talk about telling 'little white lies'. Ask the children if they think it is OK to tell a white lie.

3   Discuss if they would tell a lie to stop their very best friend getting into trouble.

4   Give the children the following scenario.

'You and some friends are playing with a ball. You have been told not to let the ball go into the neighbour's garden because it might spoil his plants. Your best friend accidentally throws it into the garden and quickly gets it back before anyone sees but it knocks some leaves off a plant. When your friend's dad comes out of the house later in the day, he notices the plant and asks you if the ball went into the garden.'

Would you tell the truth or not?

5   Give the children the following scenario.

'Your best friend has taken his dad's penknife without his dad knowing and has brought it into school. He says that he is going to carve his name under the table when no one is looking. Although neither of you is allowed in the park, he asks you to go with him through the park on the way home from school so that he can also carve some things on the trees. Your teacher sees you whispering and asks you what it is all about.'

Would you tell the truth or not?

6   Discuss with the children what kinds of situation could have very serious consequences if someone did not tell the truth. Invite the children to complete Activity Sheet 37 by writing about the possible consequences in each picture of telling the truth and not telling the truth.

7   Review the children's answers with the whole class.

Resources

Photocopies of Activity Sheet 37

Extension activities

Ask the children to think of some more scenarios about telling the truth or not telling the truth and the different consequences. Go round the class and ask the children to finish a sentence about telling the truth, for example 'I find it most difficult to always tell the truth when ...' or 'If my best friend did not tell me the truth I would feel ...'.

Telling the Truth by Althea Braithewaite, A & C Black (Publishers) Ltd.
ISBN 0-7136-4499-0

Name .... Date ....

Being truthful

If this was you, what would you do? ....

....

....

....

....

What could happen if you decided not to tell the truth about what you had found? ....

....

What could happen if you told the truth about what you had found? ....

....

....

If this was you, what would you do?

....

....

....

What could happen if you decided not to tell the truth about what you had seen? ....

....

What could happen if you told the truth about what you had seen? ....

....

....

Blueprints PSHE and Citizenship Key Stage 1 © Judy Hunter and Sheila Phillips, Nelson Thornes Ltd, 2002

Citizenship

38 This is where I live

Aims

- To enable children to consider what places and facilities there are within their community.
- To develop an understanding that some places are for everyone to use and that money is needed to fund such facilities.
- To consider the consequences of damaging public places and facilities.

Teaching points

Children need to be encouraged to look around their community and explore what places and facilities are available for everyone to use. They may not have previously considered that such places have to be paid for and that it is everyone's responsibility to take care of them. This is a good opportunity to take the children on some visits within the local community, for example to the public library, the park or a church/synagogue/mosque. Ask them to think about all the different jobs that have to be done to keep these places running and to note any damage they see that has been caused through lack of care.

Instructions

1   Make a list with the children of all the places they can think of in the local community that are available for everyone to use.

2   Ask the children which of these places people have to pay to go into or have to pay to receive a service of some kind, and put a £ sign next to them.

3   Choose from the list one of the places that offers a free facility and generate a list of all the resources that would be needed to keep that place running, including the jobs people do.

4   Ask the children where they think the money comes from to pay for the facility and what it would be like if we had no facilities in our community that were available for everyone.

5   Ask the children to imagine the following scenario.

'Your classroom is for anyone from the local community to visit and use. After a week some things go missing, books are torn, wall displays are scribbled on and some of the furniture has been damaged.'

Ask the children to consider the following questions:

- What feelings might you have?
- Do you think the people who had been using the classroom would be responsible for the damage?
- How/why might it have happened?
- What can be done to put it right?

6   Ask the children if it would be different if their public library (or their local park, sports field, museum, cinema) was damaged in such a way. Do you think the people who had been using the facility would be responsible for the damage? How/why might it have happened? What can be done to put it right?

7   Discuss with the children whether they think it makes a difference when someone has to pay to use a facility. Why/why not?

8   Invite the children to complete Activity Sheet 38 by writing down all the places that are available to the public in their local community and drawing a symbol next to each one to represent that place in some way.

Resources

Photocopies of Activity Sheet 38

I don't care! Learning about respect by Brian Moses, Wayland Publishers Ltd.
ISBN 0-7502-2136-4

38
**Activity
Sheet**

This is where I live

Write the names of places in your local community that everyone can use.
For each place, draw in the box next to it a symbol to show what that
place is.

In my community we have:

....

....

....

....

....

....

Citizenship

39 We all need each other

Aims
- To develop an understanding of how the community is supported by businesses and services.
- To consider how a community relies on everyone within it.
- To consider the financial implications of running a business or offering a service.

Teaching points
You may prefer to ask the children to look around their local area and see what different shops there are, what businesses exist and what services are available before commencing this activity. The children may need help in understanding what a 'service' is.

Instructions
1   Discuss with the children what shops, businesses and services exist in the local community and write them down. Ask them why there might be only one butcher's shop, for example, in the immediate area or, if there is a big supermarket, why there may not be as many smaller shops, etc. (Draw out that shops need to make money to pay wages, etc.)

2   Take as an example 'a day in the life of a supermarket'. Ask the children if they have all been to a supermarket or a big shop. What kind of jobs are people employed to do in a supermarket? (Make a list together of all the possible jobs, for example cashiers, shelf stackers, delivery people, packers, counter assistants, clerks, secretaries, telephonists, managers, assistant managers, trolley attendants, wages clerk, cleaners …)

3   Now discuss with the children who and what, apart from the people who are actually employed to work in the supermarket, also have a part to play in keeping the supermarket in business (customers, postperson, gas, electricity and water companies, repair people, telephone company, window cleaner …).

4   Try to draw out how one business/service both affects and relies on others. One business helps to keep people employed in other businesses; that is why when a few shops close in one community it sometimes makes it difficult for the other shops to keep open as not as many customers may go there.

5   Return to the list of shops, businesses and services previously generated with the children and discuss the range that is available and whether there is anything they feel is missing. What would make the community a better place to live?

6   Explain to the children that what exists in the community is decided by the 'local council' and that they are going to write a letter suggesting that they consider making some kind of change within their community. The children can either work in small groups or individually to complete Activity Sheet 39.

7   Send the children's ideas to the local council and ask if someone can visit the school to discuss the ideas with the children or, alternatively, write a reply to them.

Resources
Photocopies of Activity Sheet 39

Extension activities
Invite the local councillor to come and talk to the children about what they do and the decisions they are involved in. In particular, ask them to discuss with the children what they can do to help their local community.

 Billy Bean's Dream by Simone Lia, David & Charles Children's Books.
ISBN 1-86233-260-6

We all need each other

Finish the letter below by writing and drawing in your idea to help to make the local community a better place.

Dear

In school we have been talking about our local community and all the businesses, shops and services that we have in it. We think our community could be made better by

We are in Class .... of ....
.. school and would very much like someone from your offices to visit us to talk about our ideas.

Yours sincerely,

Blueprints PSHE and Citizenship Key Stage 1 © Judy Hunter and Sheila Phillips, Nelson Thornes Ltd, 2002

Citizenship

40 Being together

Aims

- To develop an understanding of special family and community events and why we have them.
- To explore the value of sharing with other people through events and celebrations.

Teaching points

The nature of community events/celebrations will largely depend on the cultural mix of children within your school. This is an opportunity for all the children to share a little of their culture with each other – perhaps you could involve parents and members of the community in organising some events within school for the children and for each other. Church schools will be able to tie in this aspect of the curriculum with an exploration of special events within the Church.

Instructions

1   Discuss with the children what special events/celebrations they can think of in which people take part as a family or community. Write these down. If a minority of the children take part in events/celebrations in which the others do not, ensure that their events events/celebrations are given as much status as those put forward by the majority.

2   Explore what happens with each event, for example how people celebrate their birthdays. Would it be the same celebrating a birthday on your own, with no cards or presents or any kind of celebration at all?

3   Discuss, as an example, how Christmas is a shared celebration for many people in Great Britain. In what kinds of way do people come together to celebrate Christmas? What are some of the symbols of Christmas? People usually gather together to celebrate a marriage. In what kinds of way do they celebrate? (This is a good opportunity to look at how people celebrate marriages in different countries and different cultures.)

4   Are there any special events that happen in this particular community that might not happen elsewhere? (Local fairs, for example). What special events/celebrations happen in school? (Sports days, assemblies, school parties ...)

5   Invite the children to complete Activity Sheet 40, which focuses on their favourite celebration and the people who are part of that celebration.

Resources

Photocopies of Activity Sheet 40

Extension activities

Prepare a class event to celebrate all the special talents and qualities of everybody in the class. (This can be done as an assembly if you prefer).

Nominate one day per year for each child during which the rest of the class takes extra care in sharing and helping that child.

The Party in the Sky by Alison Catley, A Red Fox Book published by Random Century Children's Books.
9-780099656005

All Kinds of Beliefs by Emma Damon, Tango Books.
ISBN 1-85797-505-6

Being together

Let's Celebrate!

Draw below a picture of your favourite celebration or something to represent it.

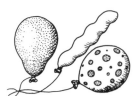

Who shares your celebration with you? ....

....

....

What feelings do you have when you think of your favourite celebration?
Write the words to describe those feelings in the balloons below.

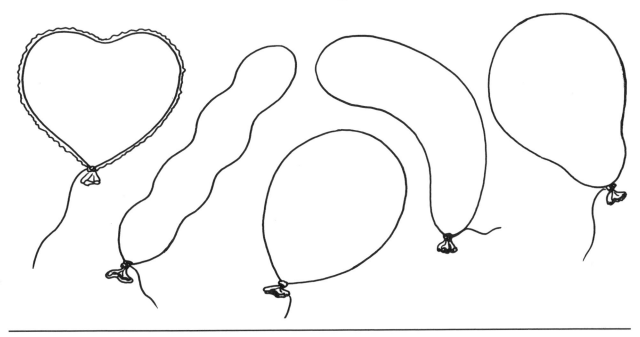

Citizenship

41 Developing the language

Aims
- To begin developing a language in relation to citizenship issues.
- To practise using specific vocabulary.

Teaching points
Feeling confident to contribute fully within the local, national and global community demands an understanding of the language that is used. If children begin to understand and practise this language early in life they are more likely to see it as part of their common vocabulary as young people and adults and feel confident to engage in debates and discussions. Select the vocabulary for this activity according to the needs and maturity of your children.

Suggested words:

community	fair	unfair
responsibility	citizen	government
respect	honesty	council (school/local)
local	national	society

Instructions
1 Explain to the children that there are some useful words to know and understand when talking about some of the issues in these lessons. These words also help us when we watch the news or read something in a newspaper.

2 Write up each word in turn and discuss its meaning. Ask the children to try to think of a sentence using the word. (You can also encourage the children to practise their dictionary work by dividing them into groups and asking each group to look up a few words and then think of sentences containing the words to share with the rest of the class.)

3 Ask the class what things they are aware of that have been happening recently in the community or in the world. Write up their ideas and contribute by explaining other significant items of which they may be unaware.

4 Divide the class into small groups. Distribute some newspapers to each group and ask them to cut out any headlines or short articles which they understand and find interesting or that are about the things they have just been discussing.

Explain to the groups that they are going to prepare a short news broadcast for the rest of the class. Ask them to decide on three or four events or stories and to write out and practise how they want to present their news to the class. Discuss how this is usually done on television. You may want the children to prepare their material on computer, watch and discuss some pre-recorded news broadcasts first, video their own news broadcasts and perhaps include a weather forecast.

5 Review the activity with the whole class. How did they feel when they were presenting their news? How easy was it to decide on their stories? How easy was it to present the news fairly and without putting forward their own views? Is it important to do this? Why/why not?

6 Invite the children to complete Activity Sheet 41 as a summary of their work.

Resources
National and local newspapers
Scissors
Photocopies of Activity Sheet 41

Extension activities
Bring in newspapers and articles on a regular basis to encourage the children to begin to take an interest in them. Start a weekly news board in the classroom and divide it into local news, national news and class news.

Video record short news broadcasts and show them to the class to generate discussion on topical events.

Developing the language

Write on the television screen the stories or events your group chose for their news broadcast.

Why did you choose these events for your news? ....

....

....

What did you enjoy about this activity? ....

....

What do you think your group did very well? ....

....

....

At home try to watch the news on television, or listen to it on the radio, and tell your teacher about any interesting stories and events.

Blueprints PSHE and Citizenship Key Stage I © Judy Hunter and Sheila Phillips, Nelson Thornes Ltd, 2002

Citizenship

42 Put it to the vote

Aims

- To develop an understanding of the underlying principles of the voting system.
- To enable children to reflect on the feelings they might experience when their vote wins/does not win.
- To raise awareness of the monetary value of resources.

Teaching points

Plenty of opportunities will arise in class and school for children to begin to develop an understanding of the democratic system by being involved in some decision-making processes. Make it clear to children what is non-negotiable and why, and what they can have some say in and why. It is unfair to involve the children in making decisions if in reality they have no control at all over the outcomes. In light of this, be explicit about Instruction 1. It must be clear to children whether they have some actual money to spend or are just pretending for practice. If they are only pretending, it may at least be possible for the children to put their ideas to the headteacher.

Instructions

1 Explain to the children that they are going to pretend that an amount of money has been allocated to the school to improve it in some way and they are going to discuss in what possible ways the money could be spent. Decide on the sum of money, for example £200. (If some money for the class can actually be made available that is even better! Perhaps the headteacher would be willing to allocate a small amount (£25) and the children could discuss what resource to buy for the classroom).

2 First of all, draw up a list with the children of all the things that need to be taken into account when deciding how to spend the money. For example: What would benefit the whole school? What resources are we short of at the moment? What would be of lasting value? How much do different resources cost? (Old catalogues can be helpful here.)

3 Divide the class into small groups and ask each group to generate a list of possible ideas for spending the money.

4 Ask each group to decide on the three ideas they prefer the most from their lists.

5 Compile a class list by asking each group to say what their three ideas are and why they feel they would be useful. After discussion, if the class agrees that some of the ideas are not feasible, agree to cross these off the list.

6 Ask each group to now discuss which three ideas they like the best from the class list. Remind them of the importance of remembering all the things that need to be taken into account when deciding and not to think about just their own ideas.

7 Write down these three ideas and explain that everyone in the class is going to vote to decide on the winning idea. Discuss what voting means and the implications of agreeing to the outcome, whatever it is.

8 Carry out the voting by either asking for a show of hands or asking each child to write the idea they want to win on a slip of paper and hand it in for counting.

9 Announce the winning idea. Review the activity by discussing the fairness/unfairness of voting as a method of making decisions. Are there some things that it would not be OK to vote on? Why/why not?

10 Invite the children to complete Activity Sheet 42 as a review of the activity.

Resources

Slips of paper for voting (see Instruction 8 above)
Photocopies of Activity Sheet 42

Extension activities

Maximise the opportunities to involve the children at times of local and national elections.

Children may vote on who is going to be the class representative(s) on the school council.

When buying classroom resources, involve the children wherever possible in discussing what is needed and why and the costs of the resources.

Name .... Date ....

Put it to the vote

Which idea did you think was the best idea? Write it on the slip of paper
that goes in the ballot box.

Which idea got the most votes? ....

....

Why do you think this idea got the most votes? ....

....

How did you feel about the idea that got the most votes? ....

....

Reviewing progress

The following activities are included to help the children to review their progress in PSHE and citizenship. Activity Sheets 43–46 can be used at any stage you feel appropriate and should be seen as either a stimulus for discussion or a review of discussion rather than as activities in themselves.

Encouraging children to work together in groups and share their learning, thoughts and ideas is an essential element of the curriculum itself, especially in citizenship and social skills development. Remember PSHE and citizenship need to be 'lived' and there are many more activities that children will take part in that also form part of this curriculum. Children, however, do not necessarily make the connections that we make as adults, so try to review other aspects of school life as part of PSHE and citizenship; even a five-minute discussion with the class can help them to begin to see the connections. Encourage the children to greet visitors and explain a little about what they have been doing in class. Follow up visits by asking the children to write thank you letters (or emails) and whenever possible involve parents/carers by explaining what their children are doing and give them the opportunity to reinforce the learning at home. Working with parents is especially important when dealing with health education issues as the lifestyle the children have at home will have a greater impact than the lifestyle they adopt in school.

Review activities

Activity Sheet 43 Keeping healthy
Activity Sheet 44 The tree of success
Activity Sheet 45 Jumbled up
Activity Sheet 46 Paper chains

N.B. Activity Sheet 46 can be adapted so that the children work in groups to make a real paper chain and either write on the links the names of everyone in their class or the names of people in the community who help them.

Keeping healthy

Think about all the things you have been learning about which help you to keep healthy. What can you remember?

Write what you have learned on the posts of the fence.

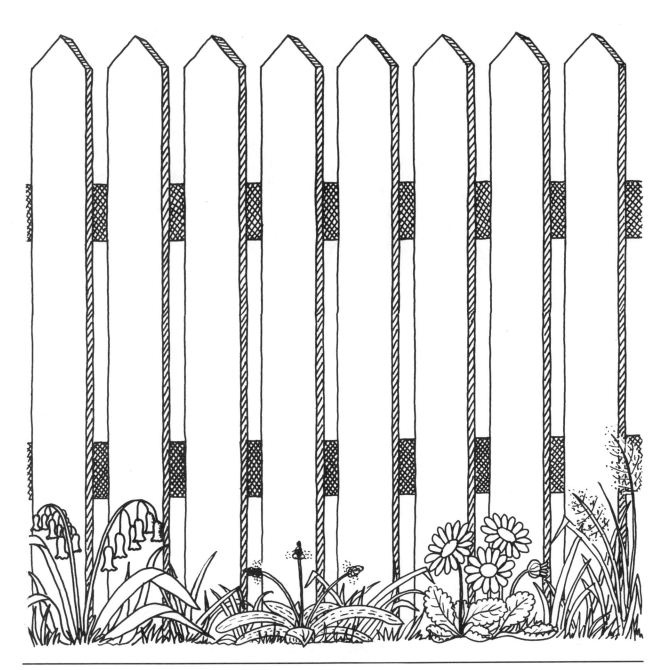

The tree of success

Each one of us has many different skills and talents. We are all special. On the tree of success below, write your name on the tree trunk. Then write some of the special things about you on the leaves.

Jumbled up

The sentences below are all messages about you and keeping yourself as safe and as healthy as possible. Write each sentence in the right order so that it makes up a health message.

1   every day Drinking is very for me good plenty of water.

     ....

2   I should my teeth brush twice at least a day.

     ....

3   exercise to keep strong and fit my body every day Doing some helps.

     ....

4   care for each other We are all part of a should and community.

     ....

5   growing all the time and I am changing.

     ....

6   special and We are all have different talents.

     ....

7   medicine only take someone I trust from I should.

     ....

8   rules helps Having to me keep safe.

     ....

Paper chains

Here is a picture of a paper chain.

Write on the links of the chain all the people you can think of that are part of your community.

Think about your family, your friends and all the people who help you in different ways.

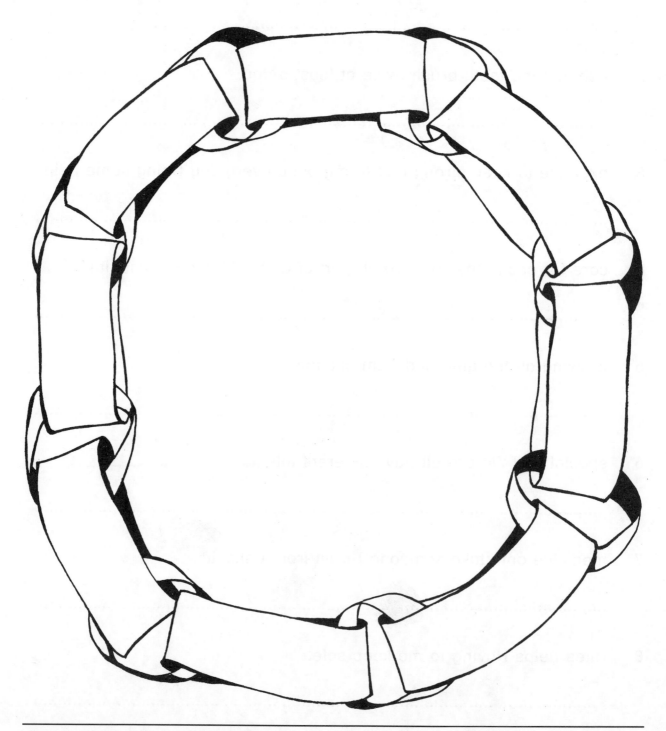